Making
Simple Needle Felts

Steffi Stern

Hawthorn Press

Making
Simple Needle Felts

Steffi Stern

40 Inspiring Seasonal Projects

Hawthorn Press

Hawthorn Press

Published by Hawthorn Press, Hawthorn House,
1 Lansdown Lane, Stroud, Gloucestershire, GL5 1BJ, UK
Tel: (01453) 757040   Email: info@hawthornpress.com
Website: www.hawthornpress.com

Cover and completed project photographs © Faisal Khouja
Photographic styling by Laura Mirjami
Instructional photographs by Steffi Stern
Design by Lucy Guenot
Printed by Short Run Press Ltd, Exeter, 2018, 2020

Every effort has been made to trace the ownership of all copyrighted material. If any omission has been made, please bring this to the publisher's attention so that proper acknowledgement may be given in future editions.

The views expressed in this book are not necessarily those of the publisher.

Printed on environmentally friendly chlorine-free paper sourced from renewable forest stock.

British Library Cataloguing in Publication Data applied for

ISBN 978-1-907359-97-2

Dedication

This book is dedicated to my friend Jan Perkins,
who is teaching me daily that life is for living,
children are miracles and crafting is for sharing!

Contents

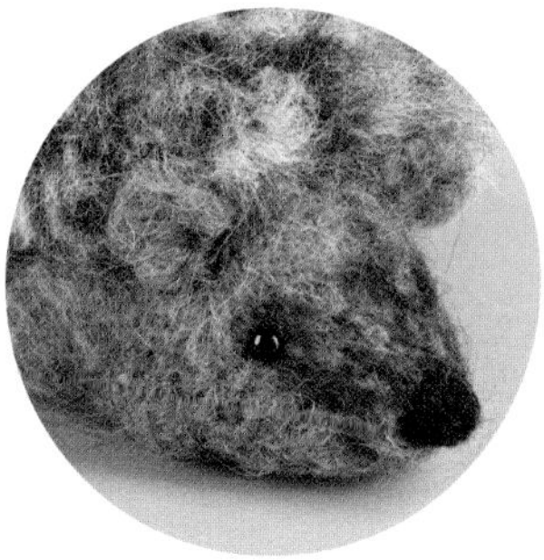

Foreword by Sarah Brown   7
Introduction   8
Needle felting in a nutshell   10
The wool   14
Tools and accessories   19
Techniques   20

Making people, fairies and angels   27

Making heads, arms and hands   28
Spring sprite with legs   35
Fairy or sprite without legs   37
Rose fairy   39
Angel   41
Tree-top fairy   44

Spring   47

Simple butterflies   48
Bunnies   50
Baby barn owl   54
Primroses   56
Hen and chicks   58
Blue tit   62

Summer   67

Dragonfly   68
Roses   70
Strawberry & Strawberry girl   72
Honey bee   76
Alder cone bee   78
Pocket mouse   80
Mermaid & Merboy   84
Pom-pom hedgehog   86

Autumn   93

Hairy spider   94
Mini apples & Apple girl   95
Toadstool   99
Toadstool boy   101
Mushroom   104
Leaves   107
Miniature pumpkins & Pumpkin girl   110
Snail   114
Acorns   116
Gnome   118
Pine cone gnome   123

Winter   127

Donkey   128
Father Christmas   133
Snowman   140
Sheep and lamb   144
The Nativity: Mary   149
       Joseph   150
       Baby Jesus   154
Robin   156
Baubles   160
Christmas pudding bauble   163

Frequently asked questions   166

Resources   168
Acknowledgements   169

Foreword

It was an honour to be asked to write the foreword for Steffi's second inspirational needle felting book, *Making Simple Needle Felts*. As an active member of the Facebook group 'Needle Felting UK' that I set up four years ago, Steffi always offers insightful advice, tips, tutorials and supplies to both beginners and experienced fellow felters alike.

In the increasingly popular world of needle felting, Steffi and her business have gone from success to success, and with over fifteen years of felting experience she is the perfect person to guide us through the fascinating world of felting. She attends many fibre festivals, offers friendly tutorials and workshops, is a craft channel star and has now written her second book. Now, along with her business partner Sophie, Steffi has extended her business online with the fabulous fibre shop, *The Makerss*.

Steffi's second book makes needle felting accessible to everyone. Full of clear instructions, colourful photos and jam-packed with advice and techniques, it's perfect for anyone beginning their own addictive needle felting journey.

My own journey began in 2011 when I attended a local felting workshop. The tutor emptied out her wool supplies and out popped an incomplete bunny and from that moment on I was addicted to the magic of turning wool into 3D creations. Four years later, Needle Felting UK has over 11,000 group members, and needle felting has truly taken over my life, and I love it!

I know Steffi's energy and enthusiasm will enable her brilliant needle felting business to continue to blossom. Her motto, 'Everyone a Maker', is ideal for this book and I know it will be loved by beginners and experienced felters alike.

Happy felting everyone!

Sarah Brown, Needle Felting UK (Facebook)

Introduction

I was brought up in Germany with crafts surrounding my daily life. As a family, with friends and at school we always crafted and created, often inspired by the seasons of the year and annual celebrations such as Christmas and Easter. As a child I used to go on summer camps where we would set up tents for sleeping and eating but, most importantly, to do crafts. I experienced so many different types of niche crafting that I never saw again until I was a grown-up and it was made popular through social media and craft TV. Knitting and crocheting was around me from the beginning as my mother was constantly doing both and even until just before her death recently she knitted and crocheted like nobody I have ever known! A childhood friend of my family ran a knitting and haberdashery shop and I spent hours surrounded by buttons, yarns and creativity!

When I had my own children it was no surprise that I was hugely attracted by the creativity of Waldorf education and for the last fourteen years my children have had the benefits of learning traditional skills such as spinning, felting, weaving, sewing, knitting, crocheting, modelling etc. I have always believed that the values of anthroposophy around crafting and creativity (very similar to my own German state school education) should be made available to all children in the world. I still believe that using traditional skills, good quality and natural materials, being inspired by nature and embracing colour and creativity are essential in childhood.

I have fond childhood memories of experiencing nature on a daily basis during all seasons. My parents had the attitude that if it wasn't raining I should be outdoors amusing myself. I remember having had a tomboyish early childhood, climbing trees and roaming the countryside barefoot. I ran rather than walked across stubbled fields as that stopped it hurting my bare feet. I remember eating fat black cherries on the top of a tree in the middle of a field, playing in streams, collecting snails and lizards, making friends with kittens and following the cows on their daily journey

from the milking shed to the fields. I sledged in winter and swam in lakes in the summer. I walked through woods, watching wild animals. I took it all for granted. After all, that's what all children do, don't they?

My own children are growing up under very different circumstances to mine. Their world is inhabited by electronics, mobile phones, computers and all kinds of indoor entertainment. I live in a world where we are afraid to let our children roam the countryside all day and where their freedom is so much more restricted than when I was a child. From an early age in their childhood I have tried to give them as many outdoors experiences as possible, allowing them to discover the magic of our everyday natural world, trying to manage the challenges of our modern world by remembering the beauty that surrounds us.

I discovered the importance of having a little nature corner in our house. This was a small space where we put our findings from our walks such as a special leaf, acorns, pine cones, flowers etc. It became a real passion of mine to create a small world that represented what was happening out in nature during the different seasons. Then I also began to display seasonal items that I had crafted myself. It was through the desire to replicate nature at home that I stumbled across needle felting many years ago.

I found that needle felting is the most versatile way to create little ornaments to adorn my version of a seasonal tableau. Many people have such nature tables or corners and they can be called many other names. The importance about the nature corner or table is that they are very individual and in my opinion should represent what the times of the year mean to each family. Some families may follow Christian themes as well as nature themes, some may be more Pagan oriented, some focus entirely around nature's seasons wherever in the world they may be.

Just have a go

If you have never heard of needle felting before or if you have never tried it, don't worry: it is also one of the simplest crafts to learn. It is rapidly growing in popularity, even though not many people have grown up seeing others doing it, and judging from the many people I chat to at craft fairs, this can make people a little reticent in trying it out. I have borne this in mind while writing the book. There are plenty of really simple craft projects in this book that will help any beginner to get started and you will soon be tempted to do more and more. I am confident that more seasoned needle felters may also pick up a few new tricks as well!

I have heard people say that they find needle felting is an aggressive craft activity as it involves fast stabbing movements. I disagree with that. I have found that the craft is very therapeutic and relaxing and quite hard to put down once started. The needle is simply tangling up the wool fibres in the most efficient way, which in turn compresses them down, pushing the air out. In the process the wool can be sculpted.

This book is aimed at both adults and children. Though needle felting involves a sharp needle, children from the age of ten should be able to create their own needle-felted decoration. I have however also included some projects that can be made with just wool without the use of a needle and therefore younger children will be able to join in crafting alongside you.

Steffi

Needle felting in a nutshell

Over the last five years needle felting has become a more and more popular craft activity for all abilities. This is partially due to the fact that it is so easy to learn. Most people are self taught either by just trying it out or watching an online tutorial or perhaps going to a workshop. I hope that this book can put into words and pictures the magic that happens when stabbing a needle into this wonderful commodity called wool!

The wool that is used most commonly comes from sheep. However, you can use alpaca or other animal fibres for needle felting. Some people use dog hair and cat hair from their pets though not all of them are suitable for felting. For the purpose of our projects I have almost exclusively used sheep wool. Over the fourteen years I have been needle felting I have preferred using wool batts for most of my animal and 3D project shaping.

Wet felting versus needle felting

The principal of the felting process is identical in both wet and needle (or some people refer to it as 'dry') felting: the fibres get tangled up and compact together, air gets pushed out and you end up with a matted felt. Wet felting causes this process to take place with the help of water, soap, heat and/or movement. Think of your favourite woolly jumper accidentally shrinking in the wash because you washed it on a hot or on a non-wool washing cycle. Needle felting achieves the felting process by the needle tangling up the fibres when stabbing it into the wool.

The main difference between the two methods is that by wet felting you can more easily make large flat pieces with fewer small details. It is therefore the preferred method for large pictures, items of clothing such as jackets, hats and slippers. As a rule, long fibres that have been turned into wool tops (or roving) are the preferred materials for this because they make a stronger felt, which is necessary if you are making large or utilitarian items. You can also combine the two by wet felting the main part and adding details with the needle later.

Needle felting is more suitable for making small three-dimensional objects, as you can sculpt more easily with a felting needle and add details to it, such as eyes, stripes, spots etc. on a small scale. The wool that works best for needle felting comes in batts and is my all-time favourite. I refer to it as the 'quick felting wool'. If you imagine that the needle tangles up the fibres, by using wool batts, the fibres are already 'pre-tangled' whereas wool tops in general have long fibres running side by side in a neat way. To tangle up long parallel fibres with a needle takes a lot longer than using wool batts.

On the other hand, using really short fibres when needle felting means that you may not be able to create a really solid core or base as the fibres don't reach far enough to tangle up together, for example Cape Merino or the Portuguese Merino. A medium length and coarse fibre works best and there are plenty about: New Zealand Merino, Mountain Sheep, Shetland, Gotland, Ryeland, South German Merino.

When is my feltie finished – and how firm should it be?

This is entirely up to you. Some people struggle to create a solid felted object that can remain soft but still sculpted. Some people make such a solid felt that it is hard in the end to sink a needle into it.

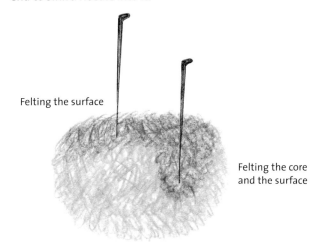

Felting the surface

Felting the core and the surface

From the very beginning till the very end, make sure that you sink your needle all the way through the whole object rather than just working at a surface level. This way, you continuously felt the centre as well as the outside of your felted item. If you do not sink the needle right through the wool (even all the way out the other side), you are just felting the surface firmer but the centre stays soft and therefore you create less shrinkage.

Scaling your objects up and down

The measurements in this book are given so that you have an idea about how much wool you need to make a certain size. However, if you are somebody who does a lot of 'surface felting' then your object may be larger. You can reduce your sculpted items in size any time if the centre has been left soft. Sometimes we want the object to be soft. There is no real right or wrong. However, if you're making a toy I would recommend felting the shape down solidly so that it cannot be pulled apart.

You can make your project smaller or larger if you wish by using the very same instructions but just varying the amounts of wool. It helps if you remember what the felting process is all about – it squeezes all the air out by tangling up the fibres. You get a good idea how much shrinkage there is in wool if you take a handful and just squeeze it into a tight round shape by rolling and tucking it in. This will give you an idea of the finished size you might achieve. Remember also that adding wool to increase the size is possible at any time whilst you are felting the basic shape. So if you want to make a larger object, add more wool as you go.

Be aware that the larger your object, the more detail you will have to add!

Crafting with and for children

I mentioned my carefree childhood and so I equally remember my crafting projects to be free of stress and pressures. I don't recall that I was ever told I had done something wrong or that things should be done differently. I grew up with a confidence in my own abilities and the belief that everything is possible. Indeed nowadays during my public talks on the subject I always emphasise that there is NO CRAFT POLICE – yes, that's right, no laws, no fines!

We need to remind ourselves as adults that allowing our children to explore their own ideas and abilities gives them confidence in their own creativity. Crafting with children therefore is no easy task! I too have learned the hard way and remember the time I sat down with my two- and three-year-olds who were meant to make pretty biscuits which we were going to show off later when their dad was home from work. I imagined that we would use cutters to create nice shapes. My children had a different idea. They created little piles of dough, half of it ended in their tummies and a considerable amount ended up on the floor. I can still feel the frustration that rose in me and the desperation I felt when I just could not get them to do what I wanted them to do. Therein lies the challenge! When crafting with children we must be aware of the following:

- For whose benefit is it?
- Why are we doing it?
- What are the outcomes I want to achieve and why – and can I let go of them?

If you are on a deadline making a perfect present for Grandma, then getting the children on board may not be the wisest thing to do.

Children often prefer the process of crafting rather than focusing on the outcome. It is often we adults who have been trained to end gain. Children do not recognise that concept. They are just as happy to craft and abandon it all when they have had enough. A knitting project that was to become a teddy's blanket turned into a skinny scarf instead! They do not yet always have the end in mind but are still free to enjoy what they are doing right now. In our crazy, fast-moving world the sentiment is turning and as adults we are actually trying to get back to the place where the process (the here-and-now) can be appreciated as much as the result. We can learn a lot from children, their free ways, lack of inhibition and capacity to think entirely outside the box.

Safety first

These recommendations are based on my personal experience and are by no means everything you have to consider when crafting with or for children (or any other people), but they make a good place to start.

1. Keep your needles safe. Have a container that can be closed securely and tidied away out of children's reach to stop curious fingers playing with them.

2. If you allow your child to needle felt, only do so under adult supervision. The needles are sharp and whilst they may not cause a severe injury, they can frighten a young child. I have allowed my children to needle felt from the age of six, once I knew they had the required dexterity to do so and relying on my judgement that pricking themselves with a needle would not upset them.

3. Needle felt and only needle felt (rather than multi tasking): needle felting is not like knitting or crocheting where you can take your eyes off and watch TV at the same time. It requires your eyes to be on the project at all times. I only ever prick myself with a needle when I am tired or take my eyes off the ball.

4. If you break a needle make sure you find the broken-off part and dispose of it safely. If the end of a needle is inside a felted object, carefully try to feel where it might be and get it out if possible. If not, do not give the feltie to a child, keep it only for decorative purposes. You may even consider disposing of it in its entirety (a hard call, I know) if you cannot be sure that it stays out of children's reach.

5. Hygiene: if you run workshops or invite friends round to your house to needle felt together, be mindful of the fact that when stabbing yourself a needle can be in contact with blood. You may decide not to share needles.

6. Use the needles correctly, making sure you have a mat as an underlay. It not only protects the needle and the table or surface you are felting on, but it also prevents you stabbing yourself. If you have the mat on your lap, make sure it is thick enough so the needle does not go straight through it into your leg. Keep your fingers out of the way. There are protective aids such as finger protectors and tools that help you hold your small felted objects down so your fingers are not in the way.

7. Needle holders: these can be crucial for people who have difficulty holding a single felting needle as the holders are far more comfortable to grip. However, having a needle holder also increases the risk of stabbing yourself or breaking a needle. The further removed you are from the work, the less control you have.

Undyed wool batts, natural undyed fibres and tops from sheep, goat and plants and natural undyed curls of sheep's wool.

Stonelamb
Natural Black

Shetland White

Lanolin Rich
Core Wool

Gotland Island

South German
Merino

Russian Karakul

Hare brown Merino

Mountain Sheep

Country Sheep

Portuguese Merino

Jacob's Stripe

Mohair

Extra Fine Australian Merino

Ramie

Blue Faced Leicester Curls

Blue Faced Leicester Curls

Masham Curls

The wool

I have been lucky enough to visit and buy wool from a local farm that keeps a small flock of various sheep breeds including Ryeland. Each year they have wool from 'first shearling' lambs, which is always softer and lighter in colour as well as from older sheep.

Once the wool has been shorn off, the farmer 'picks' the wool out by hand. She lays the fleeces out on large tables in a barn and goes through each one to make sure that vegetable matter and unusable parts of the wool are taken out. It pays for her to be thorough as she pays for the weight of wool that goes into the mill rather than what she takes back out.

In the mill the fleeces will be scoured first, which is a process where the wool is washed and this gets rid of pesticides, lanolin (wool fat) and any other residues in the fleece. Some wool felts more quickly than other wool and the washing therefore has to be done gently. Then the fleece will have to dry off.

The quality of the wool, such as the fineness (measured in microns) and the length of the individual fibre (staple) will be a deciding factor in how the wool will be processed next. A short-fibred coarser wool is more suitable to be turned into wool batts. These are large sheets of carded (brushed) wool, the fibres of which are pre-tangled though not felted. Longer, finer fibres are likely to be turned into tops or roving. Here the wool looks like a thick strand that has each fibre running side by side. This wool is more suitable for spinning, wet felting and 2D needle felting. Traditionally the tops have been more easily available though with the increased popularity of needle felting (and the use of wool for insulation and bedding) this is changing slowly.

Here follows a list of wool, tools and accessories which I have used and consider a good base of supplies to make projects from this book. When purchasing wool you are unlikely to get the option just to by 1g or 2g or even just 10g. Wool is quite cheap and so you will probably end up buying 20g to 50g as a minimum.

Batts

These are excellent for 3D needle felting, wet felting, but less suitable for spinning, depending on the length of the fibre.

Core wool

White core is often used as a neutral basic wool to start a 3D project. It is usually cheaper than the dyed wool. Often other natural colours are suitable too, depending on the finished colour of the project. Confusingly most core wools can also be used for surface cover. The idea is mainly to use a wool that is cheaper on the inside where it is not visible.

- Shetland (the whitest natural coloured wool I know), South German Merino, Gotland White
- Gotland-Island (grey)
- Gotland Lamb (light grey)
- South German Merino brown grey
- Countrysheep (variegated brown)
- Portuguese Merino (dark brown, short fibre),
- Milksheep (dark brown, longer fibre)
- Mountain Sheep (medium brown, medium long fibre)
- Russian Karakul (caramel brown, coarse)
- Karakul honey (coarse but an unusual lovely warm honey colour)
- Hare Brown Merino (short in fibre but felts down quick)
- Karakul-Merino (beige, rare to come by natural colour)
- Fox Sheep (like clotted cream colour)
- Stonelamb natural black (great black to use for animals as looks less 'deadening' than dyed black)
- Cape Merino (almost pure white, very fine short fibres and fluffy) ideal for snow and the fur trim on Father Christmas (see p 133).

Dyed wool batts

- New Zealand Merino and Mountain Sheep coloured wool batts felt down super quick.
- Especially useful is New Zealand Merino flesh pink, great for giving light flesh-coloured features to animals and people.
- New Zealand Merino, different dyed colours.
- Mountain Sheep, different dyed colours (usually a little more coarse than the New Zealand Merino).

Variegated dyed wool batts

These are often a combination of Mountain Sheep, New Zealand Merino, South German Merino and Stonelamb and the mixed colour looks more textured than a single colour, which can look 'flat'.

Tops (or roving)

Traditionally these are used for spinning and wet felting but can also be used for needle felting, though are harder to turn into a 3D shape, as the felting process takes longer. They are great for 2D felting and fairies.

Ryeland or Texel Mule

The one I use is the odd one out and a bit of a hybrid as it is processed like a top but feels more like a batt in that it is lofty and springy and tangles easily.

Jacob's brown stripey wool

This is a mixed colour between cream and dark brown and is ideal to use for the hedgehog spikes.

South American Merino flesh pink

This is perfect for covering pipe cleaners for hands and arms, and for making heads.

Multi-coloured or space-dyed South American tops

Space dyed means that the colour is in patches rather than different coloured strands running side by side. Good varieties are Cornish Seaside, Flower Garden, Rainbow and Berries, particularly for wrapping pipe cleaners and for the butterflies in this book. These space-dyed tops are really hard to source so please look in the back of the book for how to get hold of them. What makes them special is that they are dyed in patches, rather than the single colour wool tops getting mixed together where the colours run parallel.

Merino silk tops

My favourites are rose red, blue and pink, again perfect for wrapping pipe cleaners. They have tiny amounts of white silk running side by side with the dyed wool. It gives them a textured look.

Curls

You can buy curls ready made or make them yourself (see p 22). These are the ready-made variety.

Cotswold curls

Good for gnome beards and hair.

Masham dyed and undyed curls

These are perfect for fairies, fruit girls and mermaids.

Leicester curls, undyed

These are lovely, tiny, tight curls for miniature sheep.

Wensleydale curls, brown variegated

I often use these for hair, for example the fruit girls, gnomes and Joseph.

Other fibres that felt

Wool fibres are particularly suitable for felting as they have microscopic barbs that catch and hold onto each other. Other fibres are suitable for felting too but may not felt down as quickly: alpaca, camel, mohair, cashmere, angora from rabbits etc. Even your own pet's fur or hair may be felted! Sometimes it works best if you mix it in with some wool fibres to aid the felting process.

Other fibres I use
Heat-bondable Angelina fibre

You can use different types, such as Moonstone, Dragonfly, or bright pink and ocean blue. They can be used to add a sparkle or turn into film for wings.

Ramie

This is pure white and plant based, with very straight fibre. It is great for manes, hair and for making curls.

Mohair (goat) hair

This is a silky, shiny and soft wool top, great for hair and for making curls.

Measurements of wool

Knowing how much wool to use can be difficult, especially if you don't have digital scales that measure small units. I often use even smaller quantities than 1g. I refer to those quantities in the book as a 'wisp' or a 'pinch'.

What is a wisp and a pinch?

A wisp is less than a pinch and would create something tiny, like a dot. A pinch is as much wool as you can take when pulling wool off between your thumb and index finger from the very edge of a wool top or batt. This would make something the size of an olive when felted down flat, or the size of a pea when felted into a ball.

The coarseness or fineness of wool is measured in microns, which is short for micrometre. This measures the individual diameter of the individual fibre. The finer the wool the lower the value, the coarser the higher. I have not referred to microns in this book and this information here is to help you understand what microns are should you come across them. The wool batts used are usually between 27 microns (finer, such as the Shetland) and 34 microns (coarser, such as the Russian Karakul). The South American Merino wool tops are 21 microns, as are the Australian Merino tops.

Weights and measures

In Europe we use metric measurements and most wool is sold this way. But for those of you using imperial, here is a small conversion chart for the amounts mentioned in this book, rounded up or down to make sense, as the accuracy is not crucial. You can find more detailed conversions online.

WEIGHTS AND MEASURES CONVERSIONS

1g = $^1/_{32}$ oz	1mm = $^3/_{64}$ inch	1cm = $^3/_8$ inch
2g = $^1/_{16}$ oz	3mm = $^1/_8$ inch	2.5cm = 1 inch
3g = $^3/_{32}$ oz	5mm = $^3/_{16}$ inch	3cm = 1$^3/_{16}$ inch
4g = $^1/_8$ oz	6mm = ¼ inch	5cm = 2 inches
5g = $^3/_{16}$ oz	8mm = $^1/_3$ inch	7 cm = 3 inches
6g = $^7/_{32}$ oz		10 cm = 4 inches
8g = ¼ oz		12 cm = 5 inches
10g = $^3/_8$ oz		15 cm = 6 inches
12g = $^7/_{16}$ oz		18 cm = 7 inches
15g = ½ oz		20 cm = 7$^7/_8$ inches
20g = ¾ oz		25 cm = 10 inches
25g = $^2/_3$ oz		30 cm = 12 inches
28g = 1 oz		
40g = 1$^3/_8$ oz		

CROCHET HOOKS

3–3.5mm crochet hook = US D3 – E4
4mm crochet hook = US G6

Hand-dyed sheep curls, manmade artificial fibres, dyed wool batts and tops.

Dyed Teeswater Curls

Angelina Fibre

New Zealand Merino 'Rainbow' (Nine colours below)

Dragon Mix

Mountain Sheep Orange

Mountain Sheep Purple

South American Merino Wool Top 'Flesh Pink'

Australian Merino Wool Top 'Flower Garden'

PVA GLUE

Tools and accessories

The following tools and materials are a good list of essentials to invest in if you are a newcomer to needle felting or are perhaps adding to your existing needle felting materials, tools and accessories stash.

Felting needles

There are many different types of felting needles. They are in fact manufactured for machine use, which is one of the reasons why they don't appear very hand friendly. Everybody prefers different needles and they not only vary in size but also in how the sharp end is shaped (triangular, star shape etc.).

Here in the book I refer only to fine, medium and coarse needles regardless of what shape. A fine needle is usually a size 40, a medium a 38 and a coarse 36. I find that if I have those three sizes I can manage every project. For the projects here in the book it does not really matter whether they are star or triangular. The numbers I quoted refer to the way wire is measured (wire gauge). My all-time favourite needles are twisted needles, particularly medium (#38) and fine (#40). Their spiral end makes them very efficient at tangling up the fibres, because they can accommodate more notches on the end. But as a beginner you will be fine with any shaped needle.

Accessories

Felting brush and 7-needle holder

This is great for 2D needle felting and works wonders on flowers, pictures, butterflies etc. as it speeds up the felting process but also creates a smooth finish. It only works with a brush mat.

Carders or dog brushes

A pair of carders is useful for mixing small batches of colours and fibres.

Glue

Simple PVA glue in a bottle or a tube with a very fine nozzle is very useful. A glue gun is great for quick gluing

that needs less detail and delicacy, such as gluing needle felted acorns into acorn caps (see p 116).

3-needle felting tool

This is suitable for 2D- and 3D-needle felting and speeds things up massively but can also be used with just one or two needles and is therefore a good needle holder for those who struggle to hold a single needle.

Mats

FOAM

Ideally, you want something firm, like foam used for upholstery. You can cover it in hessian for extra protection and easy cleaning. A mat should last you many 3D projects – all of those in this book. It gets worn more quickly if you do lots of flat felting where you sink the needle into the mat each time. First signs of wear are usually that small pieces of foam come off or it gets thinner.

HESSIAN BAG FILLED WITH RICE OR WHEAT GRAINS

This is an alternative to the foam mat but far more environmentally friendly and can be made at home, and it also lasts much longer.

PLASTAZOTE PACKAGING FOAM

This is used in the same way as the foam mat but has an even shorter life span.

KITCHEN OR CAR WASHING SPONGE

These may not last as long but are a good emergency fall back.

Other accessories

- Glue-in eyes, 3–7mm
- Glue-in wire bird legs in black or white
- Extra-strong white pipe cleaner, 30cm
- Water-soluble paper. This should feel more like fabric rather than paper or foil and is the only one suitable for needle felting, and is great for 2D! It works well when needle felting objects, such as leaves (see p 107).

Techniques

Mixing wool

There are three ways to mix wool or other fibres. In fact you can mix wool with silk, curls and plant-based fibres, such as Ramie or similar. See the online tutorial here: https://www.themakerss.co.uk/pages/colour-mixing.

Small batches (1–5g)

Lay the wool batts or tops you wish to mix flat on top of each other and using both hands, begin to tear these apart between your thumb and index fingers.

Repeat the process of laying the wool on top of each other before the next tearing apart. The more you repeat this process the more of a single new colour you will achieve. The less you do it the more mottled and uneven the mixed wool will be. Add different colours if you want it to be lighter, darker or more of a certain shade.

The principle of mixing colours is the same as mixing paint:
Yellow + red = orange
Yellow + blue = green
Red + blue = purple
Red + white = pink

I love mixing colours that 'clash' such as bright pink and orange to make flowers, for example.

Small to larger quantities (5–10g)

You can mix wool more evenly if you use carders or wire dog brushes. The latter will not be available in really large sizes (15cm or more) but even a medium-size dog brush mixes a fair amount of wool and there really is a considerable price difference. You always need two of the same size brushes.

Lay the different colour wools you would like to mix flat onto the brush and then brush it with the other brush so that the teeth go in opposite directions. Repeat this process and you may have to 'peel' off the wool in its entirety and repeat the brushing process. Stop when the wool is mixed to the desired affect.

Drum carder (10g+)

These machines work on the same principle as the carders or brushes but the wire teeth are on two rollers, one large, one small, that brush against each other when turning a big handle. I love this bit of equipment and could play for hours trying all kinds of different mixes of colours and fibres. A small carder allows you to make one batch (maximum 40g) and I have found you have to do three rounds (take the batt off and feed through again three times) to get an even mix. The advantage is that you end up with a perfect batt as well as evenly mixed fibres and soft, 'lofty' wool.

Drum carders can be bought second hand on eBay or at wool shows but also online from shops that supply spinning wheels. Many people make their own and there are tutorials online for that. If you buy one expect to spend between £200–400. I recommend you go for quality when buying a drum carder as a poor quality one can be a pain. Quality usually means spending a little more.

Wrapping wool around a pipe cleaner or wire

  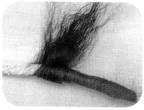 

In this book there are quite a few projects that require you to wrap wool around a pipe cleaner or your felting needle neatly, and it requires a little practice to do so. Understanding the process will help you.

When wrapping wool around a pipe cleaner it is always best to use a thin strand of wool and it will create a much finer and smoother finish if you use fine wool tops. This is why for the fairies, angels and other figures, I use the flesh-pink South American wool top for their limbs. When you wrap the wool around, imagine it is a ribbon that you are trying to keep flat. This means that you have to let go of the strand after each turn so that it does not twist in on itself (this is the opposite to how you would wrap the wool to make your own curls).

Some people find it easier to move the pipe cleaner around the strand of wool as you can keep holding on to the wool top rather than having to let go. However, this is not always possible.

When starting to wrap the wool, use the very fine ends to wrap around the pipe cleaner first as they will sink into the soft cover and stop it from slipping around. Less is always more, so use thin strands. You can always add more if necessary or just go over one area several times. Keep the wrapping tight. Don't allow any uneven or loose fibres to emerge. It is better to unwrap it a little than to ignore it. If you have to start with a new strand, secure the fine ends on a part of the pipe cleaner that will get covered over again and make sure you are wrapping the second strand round the pipe cleaner in the same direction as the first one! This is really important as otherwise you will unwrap the layer underneath. When coming to the end of a strand, fasten the loose wisps in by wrapping them extra tightly.

How to create a hard felt versus a soft finish

If you understand the process of needle felting you will know that each time the needle gets stabbed into the wool it tangles up the fibres it comes into contact with, condensing the shape and squeezing the air out. It is therefore easy to imagine that if you only ever stab the needle into your felted object just on the surface (1–2cm, depending on the overall size) it will only felt the surface but not the centre.

If you stab the needle all the way into the centre each time it will felt the fibres in the centre and on the surface. Therefore if you want to achieve a solid felted object, you must keep sinking the needle all the way into the centre. See illustration p 10.

Two dimensional and three dimensional – what is the difference?

I often get asked what the difference between the two is and so an explanation may be helpful. When I talk about three dimensional (3D) needle felting, I mean creating shapes from wool by sculpting with the use of a felting needle. The 3D sculpting in this book includes the animals, fairies, fruits etc. Usually shapes start off as a ball or sausage. I use the felting mat as support, protection for the needle and to prevent stabbing myself. For round projects I have to keep turning them regularly to felt from all directions. By stabbing the needle in strategic places I can make indentations, or 'bumps', make shapes round or pointy, make a groove. I can add other 3D shapes (arms, legs, heads) or more wool or features such as curls, wings etc.

When I do 2D needle felting, it means that my project starts flat and stays that way. The only 2D needle felting projects in this book are the primroses and autumn leaves. You can find a tutorial here – https://www.themakerss.co.uk/pages/tutorials.

Tearing wool rather than cutting with scissors

When separating wool it is very rare that you use scissors to cut it. Wool in general tears easily and it leaves a much softer edge. In this book I always assume that wool is torn rather than cut unless I specifically refer to cutting with scissors.

When tearing wisps, pinches or larger quantities of wool batts, it is pretty simple. Hold the wool between your index finger and thumb and tear parts off with the fingers of your other hand. As wool batts are generally made with shorter fibres, it is not hard to do.

This is a little more tricky when using wool tops. The nature of wool tops means that long fibres run side by side. To tear these you have to have your hands further apart from each other as you are separating the fibres rather than severing them. This also means that you may end up with a longer strand than you expected, as you will have the whole length of the fibre. You may have to repeat the process and tear it into smaller strands, even eventually tearing the individual fibres into shorter lengths.

Cutting wool is usually only done when tearing is not an option, for example, when trimming the hedgehog spikes or donkey mane. Sometimes we have to cut curls as pulling them will make them frizzy and we could lose the tight springiness that we may need for angel hair and gnome beards.

. . . .

How to make curls

Sometimes we just do not have the right colour or no curls at all. Or maybe they are too tight or too loose.

There are two ways to make curls that I use regularly. One involves a crochet hook and the other involves a bamboo or wooden skewer or knitting needle. Personally I prefer the method with the crochet hook but if you cannot make a simple crocheted chain you will need to use the second method.

Whilst you can make curls with a short-fibred wool batt, the curls will not appear like the natural curls we get from sheep. They will look more like very frizzy hair, even dreadlocks. If you want to make distinct curls, use a top or long strand of wool or other suitable fibre. It does not have to be wool. I have made curls with Mohair tops (hair from a goat) and Ramie (plant fibre). The Mohair in its natural white colour works beautifully as it is already classed as 'hair' rather than wool and so has a smooth, silky texture to it that even has a little shine like hair. Ramie is a great alternative as it is pure white, which no wool (unless bleached) can compete with. If you have coloured tops, such as Australian or South American Merino, then these will work well too. Other tops work too but the coarser the wool, the less fine and silky the curls will look.

With a crochet hook

The smaller the crochet hook, the tighter the curls. For most of the projects in this book, I have used a 3 or 3.5mm hook.

Separate a strand of wool lengthwise about 1cm or less in width. Then make a slipknot and crochet a chain until you almost run out of wool. Make sure when you are crocheting that you make each loop tight but not too tight to tear the wool or fibres.

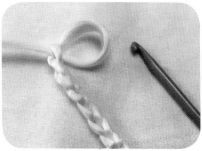

All fibres differ in that they may tear less or more easily. The Ramie, for example, tears easily. When you have only enough wool left to make a last loop, leave the loop unfinished. This means you do not pull the wool through as you normally would when crocheting a chain. We need to keep the loop open so that we can undo the chain later on. Make several batches if you need a fair amount. The angels and fairies in this book use 2–3g of curls.

Next run the little crochet chains under water to wet them through thoroughly. Squeeze excess water out of them and

leave to dry. You can speed up the drying process by either placing them onto a baking tray and put them into your oven (fan oven, preferably) at no more than 50° Celsius/120° Fahrenheit or place them on a radiator or another source of heat to dry. Make sure it is only so warm that you can still touch it without burning yourself. As we are curling natural fibres, we do not want them to burn and discolour.

Once the chains are dried (I always check that there is no damp by feeling them with my lips), gently undo the chain by pulling the loose end. Move your fingers along

pulling each loop close to the chain. You have to keep moving your fingers along the curly end towards the loops to pull them out. Again we are trying to be careful not to tear the strand or pull the curls apart. You should end up with an amazing lock that would be hard to tell apart from the real sheep curls.

You can watch a video tutorial on how to make curls here: https://www.themakerss. co.uk/pages/tutorials.

With a wooden or bamboo skewer or knitting needle

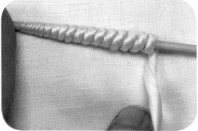

If using a skewer, you are limited to the size as they only come in 3mm widths or thereabouts. You can use a larger knitting needle if you want to make larger curls. For the projects in this book the smaller size of skewer or a 3mm needle is perfect.

As before, separate a thin strand of the top/fibres lengthwise. Fasten the thin wispy ends onto the skewer or knitting needle by twisting it around tightly. Next hold onto your strand and systematically wrap it

neatly around the skewer or knitting needle, never letting go of it, but just sliding along the strand until you run out. This way of wrapping is the opposite of what you would do when wrapping a wire armature where you have to keep the wool flat like a ribbon.

While you are wrapping the wool around the skewer or knitting needle, by not letting go of the strand, you are also twisting it in on itself, which is really important in making curls. Once you get to the end,

secure the finer fibres by wrapping them tightly over the top of the others. Then make the whole skewer or needle soaking wet as with the crochet hook method and again leave to dry all the way through, or put into a fan oven at a maximum of 50° Celsius/120° Fahrenheit or on a radiator. Once completely dry, slip the whole wrap off the skewer or knitting needle and your curls will just unfold.

Needle felting eyes

Many of the eyes in this book are glue-in eyes. They are glass heads on a strong steel pin. I use them because they are so easy to fasten in and very effective. However, they are a small part, which may not be safe for young children. If however you want to needle felt the eyes, the following instructions are simple and easy to follow.

1. You need a wisp of a black wool batt (such as dyed black New Zealand Merino or Stonelamb natural black) and an even tinier wisp of a white short-fibre wool batt (such as Gotland or Cape Merino).

2. Make two indentations with your needle where the eyes are going to go, like eye sockets. Take a wisp of black wool and roll into a ball between your fingers. Take the size of the ball from the measurements of the glue-in eyes of the each project. If the ball is slightly (1 or 2mm) larger, it is better as it will shrink in size a little when felting on. If you can (unless it is too small), felt the ball down a little on your mat.

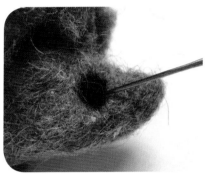

3. Then place into the eye socket and felt on by stabbing around the outside of the black ball with your fine needle, into the head. This makes sure that the black pupil stays round rather than flat felted on the head.

4. Next take a tiny wisp of white and add on top of the black. Felt down into the black until it almost disappears.

5. This is the reflection point and will bring the eyes to life.

6. You can add a little white underneath the black ball, which will make the animal or figure appear to look upwards and add expression and character.

Fusing Angelina fibre to make wings

First of all, you may never have come across Angelina fibre and, as it is a man-made product rather than any other fibre I use in this book, it may be worth explaining what it is.

It is a very thin, long (about 10cm) fibre that sparkles and is light reflective, as well as light refractive – making it also luminescent. From experience, just one fibre left behind on the table, floor, in wool or on myself will catch your eye as it is so sparkling. In this book I use it on the mermaid and merboy, as it looks like water sparkling in the sun. It is also a great alternative to add to fairies and angels, especially if making them for Christmas. You can easily mix them into wool as you would mix different colours or fibres together, as described earlier (p 20). They do not felt on their own.

  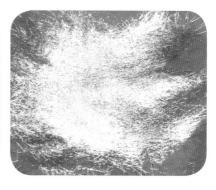

1. To make an Angelina film you will need one sheet of smooth paper or greaseproof or baking parchment and wisps of Angelina fibre. The Angelina fibre needs to be heat bondable (non heat bondable Angelina fibre is available). You also need an iron.

2. Start with very few fibres laid out on your paper. If you are making wings arrange the fibres in the direction the veins of the wings would run naturally. Lay the fibres out over one half of the paper.

3. Next set your iron onto the 'wool/silk' heat setting. Fold the other half of the paper over to cover all of the fibres. Place your iron on top of the paper, holding it in one place for about 10–20 seconds.

4. Depending on the colour of the Angelina fibre and the length of time you keep your iron on them, the colour will change after prolonged exposure to heat. The colour usually turns a warmer, more coppery tone.

5. You can make thicker film or add fibres running in a different direction, or make a larger sheet by adding more fibres to your film and repeating the ironing process.

You can also add a different colour on an existing film. The fibres melt into each other and do not bond with other materials.

6. Cut the finished film to shape. Use a soft pencil to draw on the film if you decide to use a template (below) for the wings.

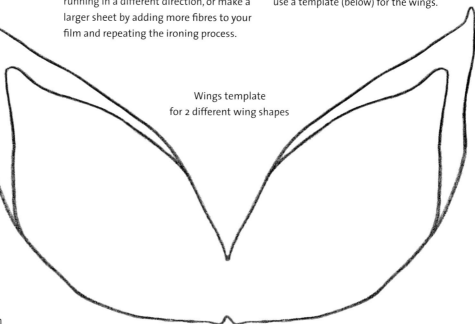

Wings template
for 2 different wing shapes

Making people, fairies and angels

· ·

Making heads, arms and hands

Spring sprite with legs

Fairy or sprite without legs

Rose fairy

Angel

Tree-top fairy

Many of the figures included in this book, including fairies, fruit girls, mermaids, merboys and people, start off in exactly the same way and so rather than repeat these stages in detail for every project, you will find the detailed instructions here. However, I do refer back to these technical methods in each project as well as give a basic outline of what to do to guide you through each step. So, whether you prefer to proceed cautiously or plunge in, you should be able to use the book in a way that suits you.

It might be helpful to know that making the head is the same for all of the projects. After that, variations apply: for example, you will use a pipe cleaner in different ways, for an angel (to add arms or make a stand for a Christmas tree) or to shape a tail for a mermaid.

Making heads, arms and hands

These are linked together here because they are formed out of one piece of pipe cleaner.

YOU WILL NEED

- 4g flesh pink wool tops (I use South American Merino)
- 3–4g white or cream core wool batts that are 'sticky', which means they don't come undone when wrapping around the pipe cleaner (I use Fox Sheep or South German Merino wool batts – I love the organic lanolin-rich version as it is extra 'sticky')
- 30cm-long extra-strong pipe cleaner (only use 1 if making hanging fairies, 2 if you are making a standing figure or a figure with legs)

Mind your needles when making figures as they can easily break if they hit the pipe cleaner. Be careful throughout the projects but especially when felting close to the wires, such as when adding hair.

Making the head

1. Tear off about 20cm of flesh-pink wool top (about a finger's width). You need to keep about one third for wrapping the hands or arms. (If making legs wrapped in this wool top, you need an extra 1g.)

2. Bend your pipe cleaner end in on itself about 2cm down from the top. Hook the pipe cleaner onto the middle of the strand of wool and secure it by twisting the end of the pipe cleaner around the long end. The wool top should be fastened securely. It will look a little like a moustache on a stick!

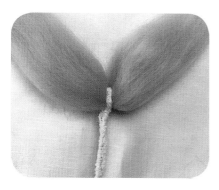

3. Move the flesh-pink wool out of the way by bending it up and away from the pipe cleaner.

4. Start wrapping the core wool batts around the top of the pipe cleaner just below the pink 'moustache'. Wrap it flat like a ribbon, which means you have to let go of the end once a full round has been completed.

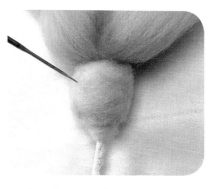

5. Build up layers slowly until it measures about 2–3cm. Using your medium needle, felt these layers into a ball shape. Add more thin layers to build it up into a ball that measures about 2–3cm when felted down.

6. Now pull the flesh pink strands from the top over the ball shape.

7. Do not worry about the top of the head where it will have an indentation or part of the pipe cleaner showing as this will be covered by hair later on. However, if too much pipe cleaner is sticking out, you can push the needle-felted ball upwards along the pipe cleaner.

8. Smooth the pink wool evenly over the white wool (remember you only need one quarter of it to look perfect as the rest gets covered with hair), then tighten at the neck and tie with a strong thread making sure that the flesh pink wool is smooth and even without any gaps or bulges.

MAKING A SECURE KNOT
Tie the thread round the first loop twice instead of once.

This will stop the thread from slipping open while you need to let go of it in order to make the second loop. This way you can tie the neck really firmly without the help of a second pair of hands.

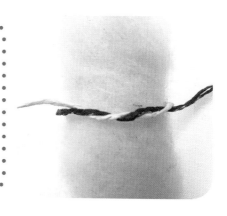

Needle felting faces

Most of the projects in this book don't have faces but I am including this so that if you want to take your projects further, you have the basic techniques.

Many people ask why I don't give fairies faces. In the Waldorf movement it is believed that giving minimalistic faces encourages the child's imagination and helps them 'project' a face onto it through their ability to imagine. I have a very practical reason here too! As the heads are made from a wool core that is needle felted to resemble a ball and then gets covered by a wool top that stays un-felted, it is very hard to then add features. If you start felting the face, the evenness and smoothness of the wool disappears. You are left with holes like pockmarks and it is hard to add features such as a nose and cheekbones afterwards. In order to add eyes, mouth etc. the head needs to be sculpted in the first place and then the second layer needs to be needle felted too. Even then it takes skill to create a young, natural-looking face.

YOU WILL NEED

2g flesh *pink wool batts (I use New Zealand Merino)

4g off-white wool batts that are 'sticky', meaning they do not come undone when wrapping around the pipe cleaner (I use Fox Sheep or South German Merino)

30cm-long, extra-strong pipe cleaner

Wisps of coloured wool for eyes and mouth

Wisps of brown for eyebrows

Wisps of white for eyes

Optional: pink blusher powder

*We have used one flesh tone throughout, but of course skin tones vary, so use more yellow, pink or brown, or pick two tones that are close and blend them together as shown on page 20.

1. Tear off about 20cm of flesh-pink wool batt, about two fingers' width. Bend your pipe cleaner end in on itself about 2cm down from the top. Hook the strand of wool batt in the middle onto the end of the pipe cleaner and secure it by twisting the end of the pipe cleaner around the long end. The wool top should be fastened securely. It will look like a little moustache.

2. Now start wrapping the off-white wool batt around the top of the pipe cleaner just below the pink 'moustache'. Wrap it flat like a ribbon, which means you have to let go of the end once a full round has been completed.

3. Build up layers slowly until it measures about 2–3cm. Using your medium needle, felt this wrapping into a ball shape. Add another thin layer and felt down as before.

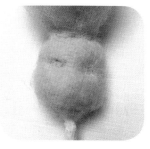

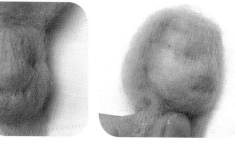
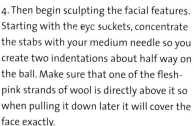
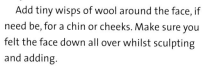

4. Then begin sculpting the facial features. Starting with the eye sockets, concentrate the stabs with your medium needle so you create two indentations about half way on the ball. Make sure that one of the flesh-pink strands of wool is directly above it so when pulling it down later it will cover the face exactly.

5. Take a wisp of the white wool and roll a small round shape between your fingers for the nose. Keep the nose small for a fairy's face.

Add tiny wisps of wool around the face, if need be, for a chin or cheeks. Make sure you felt the face down all over whilst sculpting and adding.

6. Then split a thin strand from the flesh-pink wool and lay over the face. Felt this down into the eye sockets and gently into the rest of the face including the mouth and chin. This will secure it until you tie it with a strong thread as with the heads without a face. You may find that a really thin layer is enough but if not, draw down a little more.

7. Pull the rest of the flesh-pink wool down over the back and sides of the head and felt down with your medium needle.

Tie round the neck with strong thread, using a secure knot as instructed on page 29.

8. Decide on the colour of the eyes. It is best to use a darker colour so use dark blue or green or dark brown. Take tiny wisps and add a small round ball into each eye socket with a fine needle. Add the tiniest spot of white into the coloured iris for a reflection point. It is really important that you keep the add-ons tiny. Less is definitely more!

9. Similarly use a tiny amount of pink for the mouth. The distance between the eyes and mouth should be the same, forming a perfect triangle. You can still adjust the shaping of the face but you must use a fine needle and only stab superficially as you don't want to end up with holes or misshapen features at this stage.

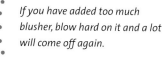

If you have added too much blusher, blow hard on it and a lot will come off again.

10. The work that is done here is of a delicate nature. If you feel able you can add tiny amounts of white into the inside corner of the eyes and some wisps for eyebrows.

11. You will find that as soon as you overdo the features the face changes. It is much easier to add features on a gnome face or make the face of an older person.

12. As a finishing touch, use pink powder blusher and give the face rosy cheeks, chin and nose. Once you add the hair, the whole face will come to life!

Making the arms and hands

There are two ways I make arms in this book. For hanging figures (Angel p 41) or those without visible legs (Strawberry girl p 72), you make the arms by cutting about 15cm off the pipe cleaner which you used to form the head. For standing figures with distinct legs (Spring sprite p 35) or a tail (Mermaid and merboy p 84), you need to use a separate pipe cleaner to make the arms.

Once your pipe cleaner arms are attached, there are two ways to complete the arms and hands. The first is when both hands and arms are covered in the flesh-coloured wool (for example, Mary p 149 and Joseph p 150).

For the second method only the hands are covered with flesh-coloured wool top. The arms are then covered with another colour wool top (for example, Strawberry girl p 72, Angel p 41, and Mermaid and merboy p 84).

Arms

1. Before starting to make the arms, refer to your project instructions as to whether you cut a length off the main pipe cleaner coming from the head or whether you use a new length of pipe cleaner.

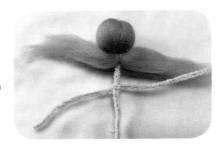

2. Move the wispy ends of the flesh-pink head cover out of the way and twist the new length of pipe cleaner once around the main pipe cleaner that is attached to the head.

3. Push the new arm pipe cleaner up so it is positioned just below the head.

Make sure that the two pipe cleaner lengths (the arms) are of equal length.

4. Wrap one of the wispy ends of the flesh-pink head wool round in front of the arm and body and then continue winding the wool down the vertical pipe cleaner.

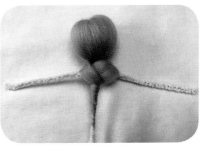

5. Wrap the second wispy end in the same way so that the wool crosses over below the head and is neatly fastened off on the vertical pipe cleaner.

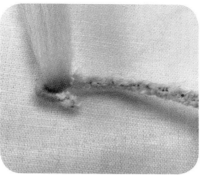

Hands

1. Use a thin strand of flesh pink wool top and start wrapping it around one end of the pipe cleaner that will become the hand/arm. Fasten the wispy ends in first, then wrap thin layers like a ribbon about 1–2 cm away from the end so you create a thin, neat and tightly wrapped cover.

2. Next bend the pipe cleaner over 0.5–1 cm in from the end so that the flesh pink cover will create a neat round end which will be the hand.

3. Continue wrapping the flesh pink wool top so that the bend of the pipe cleaner is covered.

4. Complete the other hand in the same way.

Now you have two options – check which one applies to you by looking at the instructions for your chosen project.

1. Bare arms

You cover the whole arm in flesh-coloured wool tops because you want to expose the arm (Mary p 149) or you are making a long-sleeved fairy or similar.

2. Covered arms

You only cover the hand in flesh-coloured wool tops and use another colour to cover the arm as though the figure is wearing a thin long sleeved top (such as the Mermaid and merboy p 84).

1. Bare arms

1. Use a thin strand of flesh pink wool top and start wrapping it round the pipe cleaner starting at hand end. Fold the end in and wrap all the way up the pipe cleaner.

2. Wind the wool as though it was a ribbon, keeping it flat and tight on the pipe cleaner.

3. Make sure both arms are equally and evenly covered in the same amount of wool.

 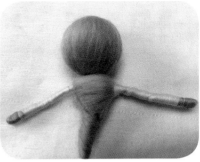

2. Covered arms

1. Start with your pipe cleaner figure with hands covered in flesh-coloured wool top.

2. Take your coloured wool and begin wrapping the pipe cleaner arms in a thin layer, winding the wool around as though it was a ribbon, keeping it flat rather than allowing it to twist.

3. Make sure you wrap very tightly so that the wool stays on the pipe cleaner without unwinding itself.

4. If your wool runs out or breaks, start with a new strand but always make sure you wind it round in the same direction as before, otherwise you will unwind the layers underneath.

Fairies and angels

The instructions for the various fairies and angels can be altered according to the seasons. You can choose between different coloured 'dresses'. Furthermore there are two types of wool that I suggest you use: wool tops work best for angels and if you like the smooth fairy look. If you are using those you may need to use an 'undercoat' as the tops can be less airy and appear flat. This under layer is usually a neutral colour wool batt.

The multi-coloured wool tops are particularly pretty – and it's harder to find a wide range of colours available as wool batts. Wool batts are more lofty and create a fuller look but are not as silky looking.

You can vary the hair of each fairy and angel. Use natural or dyed curls or use straight 'hair'. Remember you can make your own curls from straight tops (see p 22).

When you begin making the dress for the fairy you may want to bear in mind having the best and smoothest-looking part of the head facing forward. It is possible to adjust the position of the head later but usually only by a quarter turn.

All fairies, sprites and angels can be adorned with tiny decorations, such as felted roses for the summer fairy, beads that look like water drops for the spring sprites, little paper flowers etc.

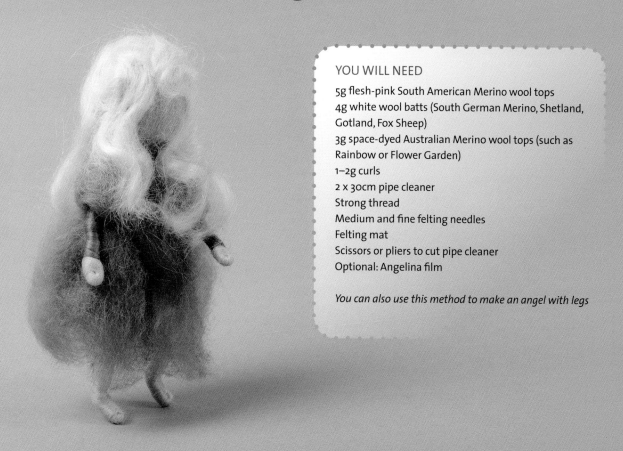

Spring sprite with legs

YOU WILL NEED

5g flesh-pink South American Merino wool tops
4g white wool batts (South German Merino, Shetland, Gotland, Fox Sheep)
3g space-dyed Australian Merino wool tops (such as Rainbow or Flower Garden)
1–2g curls
2 x 30cm pipe cleaner
Strong thread
Medium and fine felting needles
Felting mat
Scissors or pliers to cut pipe cleaner
Optional: Angelina film

You can also use this method to make an angel with legs

1. Make the head according to the instructions (p 28) and cover only the hands with flesh pink (p 34). Use a thin strand of the space-dyed wool top to cover the arms very thinly.

2. Cut a 15cm-length pipe cleaner and bend the remaining body pipe cleaner up and round the centre of the cut length. These will be the legs.

3. Wrap the body-length pipe cleaner around the centre of the leg pipe cleaner a couple more times and secure it, winding it around the lower body two or three times. Then cut off the excess. Aim to have about 3cm between the neck and the join of the leg pipe cleaner.

4. Next use the flesh-pink wool tops for the legs and starting at the bottom (foot) begin wrapping the wool around the pipe cleaner. Fold the end in and wrap it all the way up the pipe cleaner.

5. Secure around the waist/lower body. Repeat with the other leg.

6. Next bend the ends of the legs by about 1cm to make the feet.

7. For the dress, only use a short strand of the space-dyed Merino top (about 15–16cm), make a hole in the centre and slip over the head of the fairy so that the fibres are running along the fairy lengthways.

8. You should be able to gather the wool in around her waist, therefore exposing the upper arms that way. If this is not possible, the strand of wool may be too thick and you will need to make it slimmer by tearing strands off. This is best done by taking it off the fairy again. Then tear a long thin strand of the same wool and tie around her waist, pulling the dress down so that it does not bulge above the waist/tie line.

You could add fairy wings made from Angelina film (see p 25).

You can hang your sprite by attaching a thread (any fine thread will be suitable, even fine fishing line) through the top of the head.

9. The dress should not cover the feet and a bit of the legs should be visible too. If the dress is too long, tear it shorter making sure you hold onto the part of the dress that covers the body tightly so as not to tear if off the fairy.

10. Next add the curls onto the fairy by felting small strands onto the head, concentrating on framing the face first. Felt down on the top of the head, adding more strands to cover the whole head and allowing the ends to hang down freely.

Fairy or sprite without legs

YOU WILL NEED

3g flesh-pink South American Merino wool tops

4g white wool batts (South German Merino, Shetland, Gotland, Fox Sheep)

3g of coloured wool batts (I used medium blue New Zealand Merino)

1g Ramie for hair

1 x 30cm pipe cleaner

Strong thread

Medium and fine felting needles

Felting mat

Scissors or pliers to cut the pipe cleaner

Sharp scissors to cut wool

This figure is a good one if you want to make more for a mobile

1. Make the head according to the earlier instructions (p 28), then cover the hands and arms with flesh pink (p 33).

2. To make the dress, take the blue wool, flatten it out with your hands and make a hole in the centre that will fit over the fairy's head.

3. First felt the sleeves: Arrange the sleeve so that the hand is exposed, then use your coarse felting needle and stab along the underarm on your felting mat, making sure that the blue wool fits snugly around the fairy's arm.

4. Then turn it over and felt the other side in the same way. Repeat this two to three times until you have felted a seam. Repeat this on the other arm. You will not be felting the blue wool down anywhere else.

5. Next, use your scissors and cut the blue wool along the seam you have felted so that the sleeve is closed under the arm. Cut all the way to the body, giving the arm full movement. Repeat on the other side.

Use the medium needle to make sure the sleeve looks neat around the arm, covering any thin areas or felting down any wisps that are sticking out.

If you want to make a whole rainbow of fairies and string them onto a mobile, you can hang these by attaching a thread through the top of the fairies' head.

6. Now felt the cut part of the cloak that will stick out by the sides into the side of the body using your coarse needle. This will create a waistline. If the wool is hanging down too long in proportion to the fairy, tear little wisps off the bottom to shorten it. Make sure you hold onto the wool with the other hand so that you don't tear the dress off the fairy.

7. Use the Ramie for the straight hair and begin fastening small strands onto the head, concentrating on framing the face first. Felt down on the top of the head first, adding more strands to cover the whole head and allowing the ends to hang down freely at the back.

Rose fairy

YOU WILL NEED

3–4g flesh-coloured South American Merino wool tops

4g white wool batts (I used South German Merino, Shetland, Gotland, Fox Sheep)

2g bright pink Merino-silk wool tops

8g light pink wool batts (I used baby pink New Zealand Merino)

2g Ramie

2 x 30cm pipe cleaner

Strong thread

Medium and fine felting needles

Felting mat

Scissors or pliers to cut pipe cleaner

1. Make the head according to the earlier instructions (p 28); only cover the hands with flesh pink and the arms with the bright pink Merino silk top (p 34).

2. Now use three-quarters of the light pink wool batt and flatten it into a rectangle. This should be about 20–25cm long and about a hand's width when flattened out.

3. Make a hole in the middle to fit the head through. Do this by separating the strands gently with your fingers. Decide which side the face of the fairy is and put the wool over the top of the fairy with its arms by its side.

4. Adjust the dress by pulling a few fibres across the opening around the neck to cover up the chest. Next tear off a long, thin strand of the bright pink wool top (about 15–20cm), which will become a tie around the chest of the fairy.

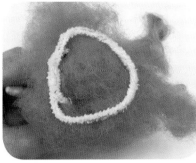

7. Then bend the pipe cleaner so it makes a circle about 4–5cm at the bottom. Once it is bent upwards it becomes a flat base and will enable the fairy to stand.

8. Secure the end of the pipe cleaner by twisting it around itself. You should have exactly the right length of pipe cleaner left to make a stand that is in proportion with the rest of the body and head. Adjust the size of the circular base if necessary.

At this point, if you want a hanging fairy, you can cut the pipe cleaner at the waist.

5. Pinch the light pink wool cover just under the arms and tie the wool strand as high as possible under the fairy's arms and around the whole top. Tie a secure knot at the front. Then use your coarse felting needle and stab it along the top of the fairy into the light pink wool to shape it and make it fit more around the upper body.

6. Your fairy still has the long end of the pipe cleaner underneath her dress. Gently fold the dress to the sides so you can see the pipe cleaner again.

9. Now use your fingers to tuck the loose ends of the fairy's dress into the circular pipe cleaner base, making sure the dress is evenly distributed around the fairy and that the pipe cleaner does not show through it.

10. Use more of the light pink and tuck it inside the fairy through the circular base. This will add volume and stability to the fairy.

11. When the inside of the dress is sufficiently stuffed, use some pink wool batts and close the base up by laying wool over it and felting it down with your coarse felting needle.

12. Continue to felt down the dress gently from the outside all over. You are not going to felt the dress completely. It is merely to secure the loose ends. We want the dress to look silky and smooth.

13. Use the Ramie for the hair and begin fastening small strands onto the head, concentrating on framing the face first. Felt down on the top of the head first, adding more strands to cover the whole head and allowing the ends to hang down freely at the back.

14. If you have any bright pink wool tops left, take a wisp and roll into a ball between your fingers. Felt these balls onto the dress with a medium felting needle as little rose decorations. You can make a larger rose for decoration (in the hair for example) by following the rose instructions (p 70).

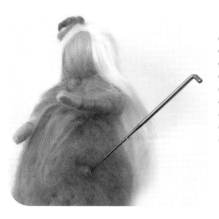

Make a tiny baby by following the instructions of how to make Baby Jesus (p 154) to make a little bud baby. Use the main colour of the flower fairy but still have the pink face and dark hair.

Angel

These angels look lovely especially around Christmas and make a beautiful present. They are a little fiddly to make and require nimble fingers and some patience. You can vary them by adding special features, such as Angelina fibre wings. You can make them any colour you like or just keep them plain white. One variation is turning them into a tree-top fairy and making an heirloom that will have that special place once a year.

YOU WILL NEED

- 9–10g fine white Merino wool tops, about 35cm long (this will be the top coat of the fairy and you can change the colour according to your liking or purpose)
- 4g white Shetland wool batts (2g more if making a tree-top fairy or angel)
- 4g of cream wool batts (I used South German lanolin-rich wool batts)
- 4g flesh-pink wool tops (I used South American Merino)
- 4g Mohair (similar amounts of Ramie or fine Merino wool tops will work too, or use ready-made curls such as Teeswater, Leicester or Masham locks)
- 30cm extra-strong pipe cleaner (1 extra one for the tree-top angel)

Optional extras:

1g of Moonstone Angelina fibre (iridescent) to make into a film (see p 25) for wings
Gold or silver thread for tying around the waist

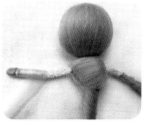

1. Make the head according to the earlier instructions (p 28). Cut the pipe cleaner below the head so that you end up with a new separate piece, about 15cm long. Use this to make the hands and arms, and only cover the hands with flesh pink and the arms with a thin layer of the white Merino top (p 34).

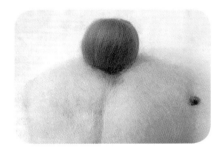

2. Next use the white wool batts and flatten this into a rectangular piece of about 12 x 8cm. If possible, have the direction of the fibres running down the long side. The less you handle it the better, so do not worry if it is slightly out of shape. We can tear bits off later.

3. Make a hole in the centre and put over the angel's head. This will become her undercoat. Decide which part of the head will be the face (the smoothest) and make sure that the longer side of the wool undercoat will hang down from below the face and the back of the head.

4. Gather the sides in so that the arms are fully exposed and felt down only on the upper body. Move the arms upwards as this will help with the next steps. Using your coarse felting needles, work the white wool in around the upper body and upper arm so it becomes tighter around the fairy's top half, creating a bodice with the lower part still fluffy and unfelted. Be careful when stabbing the needle as you may hit the wire! Make sure you cover any pink visible around the throat by pulling the wool in.

This makes quite a lovely little fairy just as it is and you can stop after adding hair if you want to keep it simple.

5. However, for a more majestic angel tear two thin strands of wool lengthwise off the soft Merino top and put to one side. These will be the ties for the top coat and the wool wings.

6. Then tear about 20–25cm of the wool top off, leaving a good length of about 15cm for the wings, then put this to one side.

7. The next step is to make a hole in the centre of the larger fine white Merino top. Try it over the head of the angel and see if you can gather the sides in as before to expose her arms. If not you may have to slip it off again and take a little off the sides to make it more narrow and try again.

8. Now use one of the two thin strands of wool you tore off earlier and tie the overcoat together just below the fairy's arms (bend them upwards if it helps) then tie it tightly, securing it with a knot. Leave the ends hanging down the front. (As an alternative you could use a thin, pretty silver or gold cord, or any colour of your choice!)

9. Next attach the hair. You can use the Mohair as it is or make it curly. For this follow the instructions on p 22. A good alternative to Mohair is Ramie and the same goes for the Mohair tops, though they are not as white.

10. Whatever hair you choose, begin with one strand and fasten it on top of the head hanging down by the side of the face, using your medium needle. Concentrate on framing the face first, then cover the rest of the head. It is important to remember that if you are using the natural wispy or curly ends of the hair, make sure you have the right length before fastening it onto the head as you will not be able to cut it. The hair needs only to be felted on with a few stabs rather than completely matting it down. When stabbing your needle into the head, mind the wire in the head towards the top as it can easily break your needle.

Wool wings

1. Take the thin long strand of Merino top you tore off earlier and the remaining 15cm long Merino top. Tie the thin strand around the centre of the larger piece exactly in the centre. These are your wings. Then gently move the fairy's hair out of the way at the back and tie the wings around the fairy following the line of the first tie right under the arms and secure, as before, at the front.

2. You can twist the wings into shape with your fingers, roll the wispy ends so they become pointy or even split each side into two and give the angel split wings. If the wings are too big, tear short strands off but be gentle so you do not disfigure them or the angel. Again as an alternative, you could use a silver or gold cord.

Use different colour wool tops for the wings, such as pale yellow, pink or purple to set them apart from the body. Use the same colour wool to tie the waist and wings. Give the angel something to hold in her hand such as a bell or tiny star. You can also add in Angelina fibre into the hair or wool before making the angel, for that extra festive sparkle.

If you are using Angelina film wings, use the template to cut them out (p 25) and glue them on preferably with a glue gun as it will stick better and faster. Any other glue will need to dry first before you can hang or adjust the angel.

Tree-top fairy

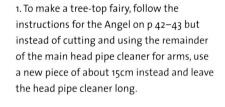

1. To make a tree-top fairy, follow the instructions for the Angel on p 42–43 but instead of cutting and using the remainder of the main head pipe cleaner for arms, use a new piece of about 15cm instead and leave the head pipe cleaner long.

2. Once you have made the entire angel (with the exception of the hair and wings), lift the top and undercoat of the angel up so that the pipe cleaner is fully exposed. Bend the end of the pipe cleaner into a loop with a diameter of about 4–5cm and secure the end by twisting it around the long end. Make sure it is tightly secured and won't come open later. This will become the base. Bend this flat so it turns into a circular stand.

3. Tuck the white top coat into the loop and cover the whole pipe cleaner ring so it is no longer visible.

4. Then felt the top coat down gently so it will hold its own shape. Use your medium needle for this.

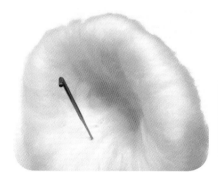 

You can make a standing angel by filling the hollow entirely with extra white wool batts and felting the top coat down gently to hold in place. Cover the base with more white wool to finish it.

5. As the angel is hollow (and needs to stay this way) you can also felt the top coat down from the inside and around the pipe cleaner base.

6. Add white Shetland wool batts to the inside to make the top coat more solid. Make sure that you always maintain a cavity inside the angel, at least a finger's length. The cavity should allow your angel to sit on top of the tree.

7. Add the hair and wings as on p 43 to complete your tree-top fairy.

Spring

· · · · · · · · · · · · · · · · · · · ·

Simple butterflies

Bunnies

Baby barn owl

Primroses

Hen and chicks

Blue tit

Simple butterflies

Butterflies are such beautiful insects and every spring I watch out for the first one that I can spot as it is a clear sign that summer is on its way. I used to tell my children a made-up story about a butterfly that would visit a small cottage garden and that it lived in a land where it was always summer. The children who lived in the cottage decided one day to follow the butterfly and got their mother very worried when she found them gone. I know that my story was inspired by the book *The Story of the Butterfly Children* by Sibylle von Olfers (Floris Books, 2009) and I loved the idea of a place where summer was eternal. I also told the story because I tried to teach my own children never to leave our garden regardless of how tempting it might be (it never worked).

YOU WILL NEED

- 30cm extra fluffy pipe cleaner
- 1g Australian Merino wool tops (Flower Garden, Berries, Rainbow)
- Pair of sharp little scissors
- Optional: needle and thread for hanging butterflies

This project does not require any needle felting at all and is a great project for children. The butterflies are low in cost to make and might be a good idea for parties or little token gifts.

1. Cut a length of 8–10cm off the pipe cleaner. Trim both pipe cleaner ends with sharp little scissors so that the fluff makes a ball shape at the end with a 1–2cm-trimmed length before it becomes fluffy again.

2. Tear off a strand of wool top of about 20cm and the width of two fingers.

3. Now fold the wispy ends of the wool top into the centre of the strand so that they slightly overlap and hold them down with your thumb and index finger.

4. Then bend the 8cm pipe cleaner in half, and wrap it around the centre of the folded wool strand, making sure that you leave about 2cm of each end at the top.

5. Twist the two ends around each other neatly a couple of times and they will become the antennae.

6. Using your fingers, pull the wings apart in the centre to make two wings on each side of the pipe cleaner body.

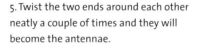

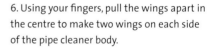

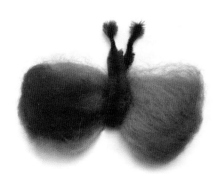

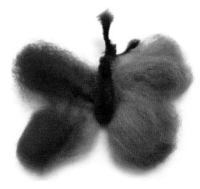

You can hang the butterflies up by feeding a thread through the two pipe cleaners that run parallel to each other. Use a needle and thread for this and, before tying the thread, make sure the butterfly is hanging evenly.

Bunnies

As a child I desperately wanted to keep a rabbit but I was denied such wishes and perhaps out of that dream I imagined how popular a little felted bunny rabbit would be for a small child. Of course it is also a symbol for Easter though often mistaken for an Easter hare, which in my birth country Germany is held in high esteem as he paints all the Easter eggs. In fact, as a young adult I rescued a baby rabbit which turned out to be a great big hare and I had to hand it over to a wildlife rescue centre. Whether you are making a bunny or a baby hare, I am sure it is a great project for Easter as well as for a child to cuddle.

YOU WILL NEED

15g of any single coloured short-fibre wool batts in brown, beige, white or even grey, such as Mediterranean Merino (brown and caramel), Milksheep (dark brown), Countrysheep (medium brown), Gotland-Island or Gotland Lamb (grey), White Gotland, Fox Sheep (beige)

Wisp of black, such as dyed New Zealand or natural black Stonelamb

Pinch of white, such as white Gotland, Shetland, Ryeland

Wisp of flesh-pink wool batts, such as New Zealand Merino

Felting mat

Coarse and medium felting needles

The bunny will be life size at 12cm in length (including tail).

Before you start, take a good pinch of the main coloured wool and put to one side for the ears.

Body

1. Roll the rest of the main coloured wool into an oblong semi-tight rugby ball shape. With your coarse needles felt the wispy ends in, which should hold the shape together.

2. Work on the rabbit's bottom first by stabbing straight into the end of the shape in semi-circles and making it flatter and rounder at the same time.

3. Then work on the opposite end, the face and head, and stab the needle from the top of the head towards the nose. This will make the shape of the face more pointy. Occasionally stab straight into where you imagine the nose to be as we don't want the face to be too pointy. Keep repeating until this has become the firmest part of the rabbit.

Ears

1. To make the ears, take most of the pinch of spare you wool you kept aside and keep a generous wisp for details on the eyes.

2. Split the remainder into two. Flatten into two rectangular shapes with your fingers. You should be able to gauge whether they are the right size as the ears will not shrink down that much. If too big, take some off.

3. Felt both shapes as follows: on your mat stab the needle into the flat piece of wool so that you draw the outline of the ear and continue to felt it flat inside that line. Lift off and fold the wispy wool ends that are outside the line in towards the centre of the ear with the exception of the end that eventually attaches to the rabbit's head, keeping those wispy.

4. Felt from the other side if necessary. Use a tiny wisp of the flesh-pink colour for the centre of the ears and felt it down so it looks like dusting.

5. Now the ears should be pretty much identical and ready to be attached to the body.

6. Lay the ear flat onto the side of the rabbit's head, the pink facing up. Stab the wispy ends of the ear into the rabbit's head so that you can let go of the ear. Then bend the ear forward and pinch it slightly so it creates a shell-like shape facing forward or to the side, whichever you prefer. Now holding it in place like this, stab the needle all around the base of the ear and fasten it on properly. Repeat with the second ear.

Eyes

1. When you are ready to make the eyes, make two indentations with your felting needle where you imagine the eyes to be. Rabbits' eyes are to the side of their heads! At this point it may help to shape the face and head a little more. You will now begin to see your rabbit becoming more real.

2. Use wisps of white wool and make two flat circles. Felt both of those into the eye sockets. Don't worry if they look large. It is better they are too big than too small. Then use two slightly larger wisps of black and roll into two same-size balls. Secure them into a good shape with a few stabs of the needle. Make sure you have your fingers out of the way and you may find that the medium needle works better.

 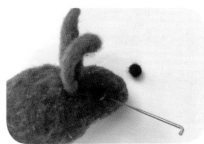

3. The position of the black eye ball on the white patch determines the expression of your rabbit. If the white shows below the black, the rabbit looks cute and subdued. If all of the white shows around the black, the rabbit looks alarmed. Bearing this in mind, needle felt the black ball on top of the white patch. Stab the needle around the edges of the black ball rather than straight on top. We want the shape to stay round.

If you have too much white showing, cover with the main coloured wool; if you need more white, add little wisps.

4. Now take a tiny bit of white wool and roll into a small ball in between your fingers then attach on top of the black ball. This is the reflection point and it should be really small so when looking at it, it doesn't stick out like a feature.

Eyelids and lashes

1. Use tiny amounts of the main coloured wool and felt loosely above the eye ball to give the rabbit eyelids and eyelashes. It makes the eye look less vulnerable. (If you have a darker colour, you could use that instead for the effect of darker eye lashes.)

2. Next, work on shaping the head some more as you have probably put it out of shape by concentrating on the eyes.

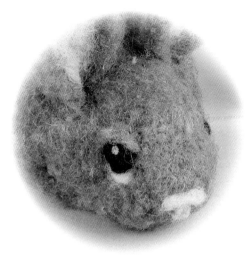

Nose

1. To create the nose, use a wisp of flesh pink and felt it straight onto the end of the face. It should look like a T-bar. Then add another pink wisp to complete the shape of the letter T. Again, make sure the face is still shaped symmetrically, otherwise work on the shape again.

Tail

1. For the tail, roll a bit of white wool into a loose ball and secure with a couple of stabs on your mat. Similarly to the eyes, felt onto the rabbit's bottom by stabbing around the base of the white ball, keeping it round rather than making it flat.

2. Finally stab the needle in a curved line at the side towards the back of the rabbit to give the impression of haunches and the same towards the head to give the impression of front legs. Repeat on the other side. If necessary needle felt the rabbit underneath to flatten it so it sits more naturally.

Baby barn owl

This is a simple project that is ideal for a total beginner. The distinct features of the framed face of a barn owl will be easily recognisable and the round shape is an easy one to make. The feature of the large black eyes, a combination of black wool and glass glue-in eyes, give the owl a cute look. I find barn owls fascinating and if you hear a hoot, then it is most likely the barn owl calling. Baby barn owls often feed each other in the nest, which is very unusual.

This comes with a warning: because they are easy to make, you may find yourself making lots of them!

The owl is 10cm high.

YOU WILL NEED

- 10g cream core wool batts (I used lanolin-rich South German Merino)
- 1g variegated brown wool batts (e.g. Countrysheep)
- 1g white wool batts (such as Cape Merino)
- Wisp beige wool batts (I used Karakul Merino)
- Wisp dyed black wool batts (e.g. New Zealand black)
- PVA glue, preferably with a small-nozzled bottle
- 2 glue-in eyes, 6mm
- Medium felting needle
- Felting mat

Optional:
- Small twig
- Brooch back (I love the no-sew brooch pins or coil-less safety pins as they are so easy to fasten on without having to glue or sew them!)

Body

1. Firstly roll all of the cream core wool up into a medium-hard oval shape, leaving some wispy ends. Begin felting the wispy ends in to secure the shape. Work on it by stabbing the needle so you end up with an oval shape with a rounded top and a flat bottom. The finished owl will be quite soft, which gives it the fluffy look so don't felt down too much.

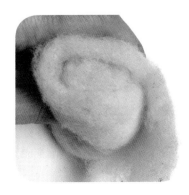

Face and beak

1. Use the beige wisp of wool and roll it into a string between your index finger and thumb. Lay the string of wool onto the face part of the owl and felt in with your needle so it makes a heart shape with a round bottom. Tear any excess string off but be careful not to rip it off the owl's face. Work on re-shaping the whole oval shape.

2. Next use a tiny wisp of the variegated brown and flatten it between your fingers. Then fold it in half and roll it into a tiny cone shape so that the wispy ends will become the base for the beak. Felt the pointy end down with your needle until it is firm and measures about 1cm. If you have too many wispy ends tear some off gently. Flatten the wispy ends onto the face of the owl, making a flat base, and felt into the area of the heart-shaped surround.

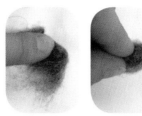 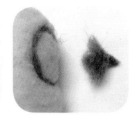 

3. Use the white wool and colour the face in. Lay a wisp of wool over the top of the beak where it attaches to the face and felt down. This will curve the beak downwards and gives the impression of a feathery owl's face.

 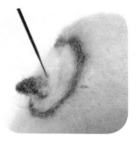

. . . .

Eyes

1. Make two round patches of no more than 1cm in diameter with the black wool by pre-shaping them with your fingers. Then felt them into place where the eyes are going to be. Keep the edges wispy. Insert your needle into the centre of the black disk all the way to the thicker top part to make a hole.

2. Sink the pin of one glue-in eye into it. Repeat with the other eye. Then add a tiny dab of glue to the back of each eye by pulling them out just a little.

Wings

1. Take two same-size pinches of variegated brown. Lay one of them over the side of the owl where you imagine the wing to be. Make sure that the top of the wing is no higher than the face! Felt the brown onto the owl, starting at the front. You can sculpt the shape of the wing as you felt it on by fastening on the brown around the edges first, tucking any wispy fibres in to create a clear contrast. It also helps keep the wing slightly three dimensional. It needs to be rounded at the front with an S shape finish at the back. Fasten on the second wing, making sure that it looks the same as the first and is symmetrical.

2. Finally felt more white wool onto the owl to cover its tummy and stab the needle around the base of the head above the wings to create a more distinct head shape.

You can make an owl brooch by using half the materials (or make two!) and keeping the owl shape flatter (about 2–3cm thick).

Place a small twig underneath the finished owl. Using two wisps of the brown wing wool, make two thin, short strands. Lay them over the twig so the ends of the strands touch the base of the owl. Felt them on so the strands trap the twig, making sure they are felted on securely, giving the impression of the owl sitting on a branch. You could use a needle and thread to sew the twig on and to secure a brooch pin onto the back.

Primroses

Primroses are such a refreshing early sign of what is to come in the following months: the explosion of colours. And the primrose has all the colours of the rainbow already. It is really easy to needle felt them as little detail is necessary to make them look like the real thing, and they come in single colours, so no mixing of colours is necessary. All you need to do is felt a small flower head consisting of five hearts all close together in a bright rainbow colour, add a little yellow in the centre and then put them together into a collection of the same colour. They cannot be mistaken for anything other than primroses!

Each primrose measures 4.5cm across

YOU WILL NEED

- 10g wool batts, 2g for each flower (New Zealand red, golden yellow, light yellow, purple, bright pink, indigo and Mountain Sheep orange)
- Wisp of extra yellow wool batts for the centre (such as the golden yellow)
- 10 x 10cm water-soluble paper
- Template
- Felting mat
- Coarse felting needle
- Pencil
- Sharp scissors
- 7-needle tool and brush mat (optional)

Primrose template

1. Using the template (above), draw the primrose shape onto the water-soluble paper using a pencil. Though we are using water-soluble paper, we are not going to dissolve it at the end but keep it in as a part feature of the flower. If you look carefully at primroses, they in fact have a little white rim around the outside of the petals. The water-soluble paper adds that detail nicely.

2. Fill the drawn flower shape in by laying wisps of a single-coloured wool inside and felt down. Fill in little by little adding more wool and felting it down. Do not worry too much about being too precise sticking to the outer line. In fact if you 'overshoot' it is better than not 'colouring in' enough. Make sure the wool is felted down firmly. Use the 7-needle tool and brush mat for speed if you have one to hand.

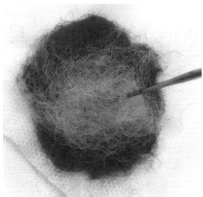

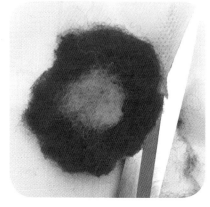

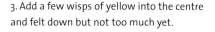

3. Add a few wisps of yellow into the centre and felt down but not too much yet.

4. Now using your scissors, cut out the flower following the pencil line. This is an opportunity to neaten up the outer edges.

5. Then felt down the yellow in the centre some more until the flower folds in on itself as if it is trying to close up a little. Your first flower is finished. Repeat and make a minimum of five of the same colour for each clump of flowers.

Hen and chicks

We have kept chickens since our children were little and although they contribute to the destruction of our garden (along with the children and the dogs), they hardly ever die in a peaceful manner, need cleaning out regularly and require us to be around in the mornings and evenings, they have been one of our best pets ever. They are little characters with personalities of their own, are used to being carried around and are tame and friendly. And they lay eggs! These little needle-felted hens will be a joy for every child as he or she discovers the hidden chicks inside!

The chicken is 10cm long and 5cm high.

YOU WILL NEED

For 1 hen and 4 chicks

6g chicken-coloured wool batts such as Gotland or Shetland for white hens, Fox Sheep for a beige hen, rust brown New Zealand Merino, muted orange New Zealand Merino for a red hen

Wisps of yellow, red, flesh pink and black wool batts (I use New Zealand Merino)

Extra for chicks: Pinch of white or beige wool batts (Fox Sheep, Shetland, South German Merino)

1 x 30cm extra-strong pipe cleaner

3mm glue-in eyes in black or amber (optional)

Glue

Coarse, medium and fine felting needles

Felting mat

Hen

Body

1. First twist one pipe cleaner end so that you make a circle of about 4cm diameter. Secure by twisting the end around the pipe cleaner. This will be the base of the chicken and will turn into the secret hideout of the chicks.

2. Bend the remainder of the pipe cleaner (still attached to the ring) up by about 3–4cm and fold over on itself (tail) making a straight line parallel across on top of the circular stand. Then bend the remaining end up (about 3–4cm). The latter will become the neck and head.

3. Take a pinch of the main coloured wool and wrap strands around the neck along the straight body and around the tail. The layer should be fairly thin but should cover these parts of the pipe cleaner. Next add more layers especially around the body and tail. The neck and head of the chicken should be thinner than the tail.

4. Now use a larger amount of wool, about the size of the palm of your hand and wrap the chicken up by laying the wool over the top so that the ends fit into the ring underneath the chicken.

5. Tuck these in and using your coarse needle begin felting this 'top coat' into the body and around the base, making sure that the cavity created by the ring is kept at maximum size.

6. Felt into this cavity too to fasten the wool. Add more layers where necessary to fatten the chicken up and cover any evidence of the pipe cleaner, always ensuring the cavity stays big.

· ·

Wings

1. To make the wings, take two pinches of the main coloured wool and a much smaller amount of white wool. Mix the two colours together to create a variegated new colour that is mostly the colour of the chicken but has white bits in it (for how to mix wool see Techniques, p 20).

2. Split this into two equal parts. With your fingers, fold in the wispy edges and lay onto the side of the chicken. They should measure about 30mm. Felt around the edges first before giving it a few stabs in the centre so that the wings stay slightly raised.

Comb and wattle

1. To make the comb and wattle, use your wisp of red wool and holding it flat on your mat, work into a piece of felt. Make sure you keep turning it over and avoid stabbing the needle too deeply into the mat as this will fasten it onto the mat more quickly. Once it is a solid but thin piece of felt cut through the middle.

2. Use one half for the comb by cutting a half circle of about 1cm length and the other half by cutting a number 8 with a fat centre of about 2cm length. This will become the wattle. Felt the latter piece onto the chicken's chin by stabbing your needle into the centre of the piece. After a while

the two flaps will automatically come down rather than sticking out to the side.

3. Pull a few wispy ends out of the straight edge of the comb and use those to fasten the red comb on top of the chicken's head slightly leaning towards the face

Beak

1. For the beak, use a small wisp of yellow and twist one end with your fingers into a tiny cone shape. Keep the other end fluffy.

2. Use your medium or fine needle and felt the cone shape down so it becomes firmer and more distinct. Chickens have a curved beak rather than a straight one so bear that in mind whilst felting the shape.

3. Use the fluffy ends (you may have to tear some off) to felt onto the face of the chicken right underneath the comb.

Eyes

1. To make the eyes, felt two round patches for the eyes from small wisps of the flesh pink wool only a little larger than the glue-in eyes. If you have chosen to use the glue-in eyes, make a hole with your felting needle by poking it into the centre of one of the flesh pink patches all the way across to the other until your needle's thicker end part has come through. This way you make a large enough hole to insert the pins of the eyes in. Check that they are symmetrical before adding a tiny dab of PVA glue behind the glass head.

2. If you have decided to needle felt the eyes then add a tiny wisp of black to each eye, leaving the paler patch still like a ring on the outside. Add an even tinier wisp of white as a reflection spot (see also how to needle felt eyes in the Technique section, p 24).

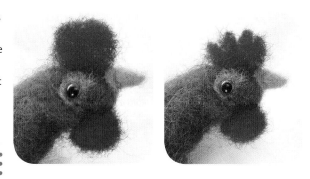

To finishing off, you could cut into the comb to make it look more jagged.

Chicks
(makes 4 chicks)

Body

1. Lay wisps of the yellow wool on top of the main coloured wool (total weight 1g) and mix between your index fingers and thumbs by tearing it apart, laying it on top of each other again and tearing apart again. Repeat until you have a mottled white yellow mix, which resembles the colour of real chicks. Split this into four equal parts.

2. Take one part and roll tightly into an oval. Felt down the wispy ends with your medium needle so it holds its shape and then felt a flat surface, which will be the base for the chick. Felt the rest down so that the shape remains an oblong shape.

3. Use a tiny wisp of orange or rust brown and felt into a beak straight onto the chick. The scale is so small that you don't need to make the shape separately first. Then felt two tiny wisps of black into the side of the head for eyes. Finally use a little yellow to make tiny impressions of wings. Your chick is finished.

4. Fit your chick inside the hen and see how it compares in size and if another three chicks will fit. If not, make the next chicks smaller or add a little wool onto the base of the hen so that she is raised more off the ground, therefore increasing the cavity for the chicks.

Blue tit

My heart always rejoices when spring is just around the corner and you can hear the loud chorus of birdsong in the mornings again! Such a sure messenger of lighter and warmer days to come and what is sweeter than seeing the birds busying themselves to get their nests ready for their babies.

This blue tit is a very simple way to make a more stylized bird (similar to the robin in this book) and looks particularly attractive when there are a few. The legs are optional as they look just as nice sitting flat.

This is a good generic shape for other small garden birds.

The blue tit is 7cm tall, including legs, and 8cm long, including the tail.

YOU WILL NEED

8g white wool batts (I used Shetland or Gotland)

1g light yellow wool batt (I used New Zealand Merino light yellow)

2g blue wool batts (I used New Zealand Merino medium blue)

Wisp of dark brown wool top for the beak

Wisp of green wool batts (such as New Zealand Merino batts Forest Green or Variegated Green) for the wings

Pair 6mm glue-in eyes

Optional:

Wire bird legs (5cm)

Wisps of medium to dark green, wisps of black for needle felted eyes.

Coarse and medium felting needles

Foam mat

Glue

Body

1. Take most of the white wool, keeping just a small pinch aside for possible patching up later on. Roll this into a medium-firm ball. You should be able to squeeze it still but it needs to be firm enough so you can stab a needle into it. If in any doubt go for a tighter ball.

2. Using your coarse needle, start by stabbing the loose wisps into the ball so that it will hold its own shape. The ball should measure about 6–7cm in diameter now.

3. Stab the ball all over to make it firmer and cover with the remaining white wool if there are uneven parts or cracks. If not, still use up all the wool. The ball should shrink down by a maximum of 1cm.

4. Now take your yellow wool and keeping a wisp aside in case you need it later, flatten into a round shape with your fingers. Use your coarse needle and give the yellow wool a few stabs on your mat to flatten it down further, maintaining the flat shape by felting it slightly down and giving it neater edges. Fold any excess wool inward around the edges and felt down. Keep lifting it off the mat to work both sides but also to stop it from getting felted onto the mat.

5. Then lay the yellow disc onto the white ball and felt down with your coarse needle onto the white surface. Now make a slightly larger blue disc in the same way. Remember also to keep a little blue aside for patching up later if necessary.

6. Attach the blue onto the white ball about 2cm above the yellow. Only felt down about 3–4cm of the blue right above the yellow. Leave the sides (wings) and back

(tail) unattached at the moment. Next pull one side carefully down so that it almost touches the yellow and felt down in a curved shape like a wing would be. Repeat on the other side. If you have created a thin patch, use the spare blue to cover up.

7. Felt more of the blue top onto the white but still leaving the back open. Next pull with your fingers a little blue outwards where you imagine the tail would be.

Tail

1. Fold the blue so that it makes a pointy end but with a flat edge of about 2cm. You may have to tease it out with your fingers slightly. Use your mat and lay the pointy tail end onto the mat and felt down with your coarse needle. Turn over to felt from both sides. You may need to cover some thin patches with the wisps of blue you kept aside or maybe to even out some unsymmetrical areas. Shape the bird all over to make a neat symmetrical shape. Also pull some of the white wool out, if you can, just below the tail and felt along the inside of the blue in sympathy with the tail shape.

2. As we only have a soft shape, now is the moment to turn the ball into more of its finished shape. Start by making the side of the head flatter or smaller by stabbing your needle into the 'eye' area.

3. Next flatten down the back by stabbing your needle along the blue from head to tail. You may find that you need to change to your medium needle now when giving the bird an all-round makeover.

Head

1. Use the dark-brown wool and tear a short and thin strand off (about 5cm long) to make the bird's eye line or mask. Felt this down neatly in the white area between the blue and yellow (face). Then add another tiny strip to go down from the middle of the brown where the yellow starts.

Beak

1. For the beak, take a wisp of dark brown wool. Flatten it with your fingers and fold in half. Then roll it up so the straight folded edge becomes the pointy end of the beak and the opposite end stays fluffy. Felt down with your medium needle on your mat into a pointy small beak of 1cm long.

2. Then using the wispy ends, open these up and felt down onto the bird in line with the eye position on top of the brown mask stripe. You can reduce the beak in size by

stabbing your medium needle lengthways into the beak towards the face.

Eyes

1. Use your coarse needle and sink it all the way from one eye across the head to the other side and move in and out a few times making sure the needle goes in all the way to the shaft/end. The eye is positioned on the side of the head right on top of the brown stripe.

2. Using your felting needle to poke across the head will create two big holes where

the pins of the glass eyes can sink in. Check they are symmetrical before applying a dab of glue to fasten them in.

3. If you want to needle felt the eyes, take two equal wisps of the black wool and turn into two equal balls by first using your fingers and then giving it a few stabs with your needle. The size of each eye before fastening onto the bird should be no larger

than 8mm. Secure the black ball onto the bird on top of the brown stripe to the side of the head by stabbing a few times around the base of the ball, therefore keeping it round rather than flat.

4. Repeat on the other side then add a tiny wisp of white for a reflection point.

Legs

1. If you are not using wire legs, felt the bottom of the bird flat so it can sit without falling over. If you are using legs, take them and bend the top half of the leg in towards the toes. Then make two holes toward the tail of the bird underneath as follows: the bird gains his stability by the bend in the legs going forwards into the body. Therefore when making the holes, use your coarse felting needle and insert it at an angle towards the front of the bird.

2. Gently wiggle the needle around and also pull it out and push it in a few times, though not all the way out. Then try putting one of the legs in. Repeat on the other side.

3. Remember the legs are bendable so if they are not straight you don't have to change the hole. Just bend the legs. Put a little dab of glue on each hole, insert the legs and leave your bird to dry standing on the legs. Do not move until you are certain the glue has dried.

4. You can add a little yellow wool if you have some available still to cover the join between the legs and the body and give the impression of tiny 'bloomers'.

5. The wire legs are very versatile. Not only can you bend them but you can also decorate them by painting them with acrylic paints or wrapping florist tape around, as well as shortening them with wire cutters if need be.

Wings

1. If you have a little green wool, add it to the wings by making a sickle moon shape about 1cm above the blue wing line.

Summer

· ·

Dragonfly

Roses

Strawberry & Strawberry girl

Honey bee

Alder cone bee

Pocket mouse

Mermaid & Merboy

Pom-pom hedgehog

Dragonfly

I love to see dragonflies around our pond in the summer and am always amazed at their size and how they stay in the air. I also love the way their wings and bodies vary in colour. I have always wondered how the wings could be made and was delighted to have found heat-bondable Angelina fibre.

YOU WILL NEED

30cm extra-strong pipe cleaner (makes three dragonflies)
1g Australian Merino top Flower Garden
1g Heat bondable Angelina fibre, 'Dragonfly'
Electric iron
Glue
Optional: fine felting needle

The dragonfly measures about 8cm in length

Body

1. Use a thin strand of the wool top and wind it like a ribbon round the pipe cleaner end, keeping the wool flat and not twisted. Make sure it is so tight that it stays on the pipe cleaner without unwinding itself.

2. Start at one end and 1cm in, bend the pipe cleaner in on itself. Then carry on wrapping the wool, also going over the bent pipe cleaner end to cover it. When you run out of wool, secure the wispy ends.

3. Then use another strand and start at the other end, also bending the end in on itself. First cover the pipe cleaner evenly then build up bulk towards one end about one third down. This is to make a body.

4. If your wool runs out or breaks, just start with a new strand but always make sure you wind it round in the same direction as before, otherwise you will unwind the layers underneath. Keep it tight!

The shape should slightly resemble a helicopter with a narrow tail and a bulkier front.

Wings

1. Make Angelina film by following the instructions in the Techniques section (p 25). Draw on the film using the template (below) for the wings and cut the wings out. You can now glue the wings on top of the dragonfly where the larger body is or you can add a tiny strand of wool by laying over the top of where the two wings meet and felt down with a fine needle first on each side of the Angelina film straight into the wool body. Then give it a few stabs on top of the wool and film.

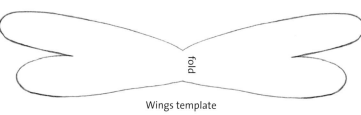

fold

Wings template

Roses

Roses seem to be significant in my family. My mother loved roses and her name was Rosita, or Rosie as her friends called her. I love them too, especially when they are scented. My great-grandfather was a trader of rose oil and travelled through many countries. It seems only natural therefore to include these beautiful flowers in this book.

These needle-felted roses look best when using variegated wool. You can mix your own wool by using two colours. See more details for mixing wool in the Techniques section (p 20).

YOU WILL NEED

1g mixed wool (try mixing New Zealand red with pink or orange) or Merino silk Fairy mix, or ready mixed batts (see suppliers at the back of the book)
Pinch of green (I used Mountain Sheep lichen green but New Zealand mix variegated green is good)

This makes 2 roses, measuring 3–4cm without the leaves

You can make several roses and decorate a tree or branches or make them into brooches.

Petals

1. Lay a strand of approx. 10 x 5cm of your main wool flat onto your felting mat and stab into it with your coarse needle to create a flat piece of felt. Lift the piece off the mat at regular intervals to stop it from fastening onto the mat.

2. Needle it on both sides. The size will reduce and it will become more solid. Make sure you keep the piece thin and even. Fold in the wispy edges but keep the ends fluffy.

3. When it holds its own shape and has become a felted sheet, fold it in half lengthways. It will measure about 1.5cm in width. Give this piece a few stabs so that the two halves are joined together.

4. Then felt one end in on itself by about 1–2cm to get rid of the wispy ends. Now continue rolling it very tightly into itself like a snail's shell but at the same time twist the felt ribbon in on itself.

5. You can felt it a little as you go but it should be fine to secure at the very end once you have made the rose bud.

6. When rolled up you can gently stab the needle into the wispy end to felt it down and to stop it from rolling open again.

7. Stab the rose into the back to secure it and flatten it down without destroying the pretty front. You should be able to see the rolled layers. The rose should be 3–4cm wide and 1.5cm deep.

Leaves

1. Lay your green wool flat on your mat. Use your coarse needles and begin shaping it into a long flat piece about 8cm long. Fold in the ends so they become pointy. Remember to lift the whole strand off the mat regularly and felt from both sides.

2. Then stab the needle sideways into the centre to continue making a leaf shape. You are making two leaves at the same time. When you have created a firm felt, use your coarse needle and fasten with a few stabs onto the back of the rose.

You can also make your leaves following the autumn leaves instructions (p 107) to create a finer finish and more authentic-looking leaf.

Strawberry & Strawberry girl

Strawberries are such a sure sign that summer has arrived. I have particularly fond memories of the little wild strawberries that used to grow in my grandparents' garden and the utter delight I had eating them. Even up to this day I am still astonished how a tiny fruit can hold such flavour. They are a lovely plant to grow for children in the garden as the strawberries play hide and seek. One day you see none, the following day you see something red peeping out from under a leaf.

YOU WILL NEED

For the strawberry fruit (about 5cm tall)

3g red wool batts (I used New Zealand Merino red)
Generous pinch (just under 1g) of green wool batts
(I used Mountain Sheep lichen green but you can also
New Zealand pale green, forest green or pea green and
variegated green)
Coarse and medium felting needle
Felting mat
Pair of sharp little scissors

Berry

1. Take your red wool batt and roll the wool into as tight a ball as you can. This will also give you an idea of the finished size. Fasten the loose fibres at the end of the rolled up ball by stabbing the coarse felting needle into them. It should now hold its own shape. Decide which part is going to be pointy and which is going to be the rounder top.

2. For the pointy end, concentrate the stabbing of the felting needle from the centre of the ball towards the pointy end, going in straight lines sideways into the red, meeting at the point. For the rounder end, run your needle in a semi-circle around the shape going straight into the top. Continue firming the strawberry up by felting all over.

3. Decide on the shape of your strawberry: Some are flatter, some really round, some more heart shaped. If you need to shorten the shape, stab your needle at a shallow angle at the sides of the pointier part of the strawberry. If you need to lengthen it, stab at a right angle into the sides. You can also try and pull it longer with your fingers.

4. Take a tiny wisp of green and lay this over the pointy end and felt on with your medium felting needle. It should look like a dusting.

5. Roll tiny balls of the same colour wool between your fingers to make the seeds.

6. When fastening the seeds onto the strawberry in random order, pick them up with the felting needle, position them on the strawberry and felt down. You may have to felt around the green to re-adjust the red which inevitably will have been put out of shape. Keep shaping the strawberry as you go along. Felt the spots all over the strawberry, smaller ones at the pointy end, larger ones toward the round end.

Leaves and stalk

1. Take three small pinches of the green wool and felt each of them on your mat into an oblong flat shape. Fold in the wispy ends and felt down using your coarse needle. Make sure that you lift the shape off the mat regularly and felt from both sides. Each strip will form two leaves. Stab the needle at a shallow angle and do not sink it into the mat more than 5–10mm to get a smoother finish.

2. Felt the leaves onto the top of the strawberry, only fastening them on in the centre. The leaves will look a little fuzzy but don't worry about that now.

3. To make the stalk, fold a wisp of the green in half and roll one end into a thin sausage, keeping the opposite end fluffy. Felt the stalk down with your medium needle and flatten out the wispy ends to form a base to attach to the top of the strawberry on top of the leaves. Felt down with your medium needle.

4. Finally use sharp little scissors to cut the fuzz off around the leaves to make them more pointy and neater edged.

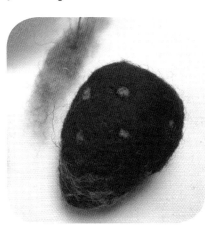

Strawberry girl

YOU WILL NEED

For the strawberry girl (about 8cm tall)

12g white wool batts (e.g. South German Merino, Shetland, Gotland, Fox Sheep)

1g red wool tops (e.g. Merino Silk Mix 'Rose')

6g red wool batts (I used New Zealand red)

1g green wool batts (I used New Zealand Merino mix variegated green or Mountain Sheep lichen green)

2g of green curls (I used Masham hand dyed curls)

30cm extra-strong pipe cleaner

2g of flesh-pink wool top (I used South American Merino flesh pink)

Strong thread

Felting mat

Coarse, medium and fine needles

Scissors

Body

1. Follow the instructions of how to make a head (p 28). Use the white or off-white wool batts for the head and cover with flesh pink wool tops.

2. You can cut 15cm off the main pipe cleaner for arms and use the flesh pink wool tops to cover the hands. Then wrap the red wool top (e.g. Silk/Merino 'Rose') in thin layers around the arms all the way to the top of the arm; repeat on the other side.

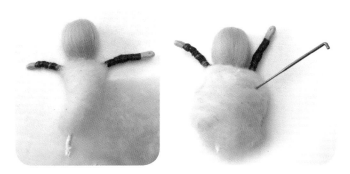

3. Build up bulk by wrapping white wool batts around the remainder of the pipe cleaner, bending it in a little at the bottom or even cutting a length off to keep within proportions.

4. As we are trying to make the shape of a strawberry, which is usually bulkier at the top, build layers of the wool to reflect this. Keep felting the layers down with your needle as you go and add more if needed. Bend the arms upwards out of the way.

5. Now add your red wool onto the white round shape by taking small quantities and laying it from the top down to the bottom, only covering small sections lengthways. Felt this down with your medium needle, stabbing the needle in from top to bottom. Cover the whole shape all the way to the head, under the arms and over the top of the arms (you will have to bend them down to do this) so that no white or flesh pink is visible.

6. Cover the bottom too and felt it flat, so that the strawberry girl can stand without toppling over.

7. Next use wisps of the green wool and lay a very thin layer onto the lower part of the strawberry. This is meant to be like a dusting and should look as though the strawberry has a little ripening to do. Felt this on gently with your medium needle.

Seeds

1. Then make seeds by rolling up lots (I made about 25) of tiny balls between your fingers in the same green wool. These are felted onto the red in a random order but with larger seeds towards the top and smaller ones towards the bottom. I find it easiest to perch the tiny ball on top of my felting needle and position it onto the red, then felt down. You may find that you have to felt the red wool around the green to adjust any indentations that you have made.

Leaves

1. Use a small pinch of the green wool and felt it on your mat into a leaf shape by flattening the wool and stabbing the shape with your medium needle. Fold in the wispy edges and lift off the mat regularly and with your fine felting needle felt it on both sides until it has become a piece of felt/fabric. It works best to only apply shallow stabs at a low angle. This way the wool felts in on itself rather than just into the mat.

Make two leaves and fasten onto the neck of the strawberry only attaching one end, leaving the leaves free to form a 'collar'.

2. Decide which the best or smoothest part of the head is and turn it to the front. You can turn the head by no more than 45 degrees.

Hair

1. Lay one strand of green curls over the head and start fastening them into the head. Concentrate on framing the face before covering the rest of the head.

Honey bee

Never has there been so much talk about the importance of bees to our eco system as now. Bees are threatened by modern farming and the use of pesticides, the disappearance of meadows and green land, climate change and other environmental factors that are contributing towards the bees' decline. We cannot draw enough attention to the preservation of this brown and yellow busy worker that is responsible for most of our food supplies around the world as one of the major pollinators. I would like to echo so many organisations by raising awareness of bees and hope that many of the bees here will be made as a symbol of life itself. I also happen to live just outside the town of Stroud in Gloucestershire that became the first Bee Guardian town in the UK in 2011.

YOU WILL NEED

For the honey bee (about 7cm long)

4g dark brown wool batts (I use Mountain Sheep or Portuguese Merino)

Wisps of yellow (I used Dormouse ochre New Zealand Mix)

Wisp of white extra fine Merino top (Ramie or other white wool tops should also work), for wings

Alternative wings:

Pinch of 'Moonstone' Angelina fibre

Medium felting needle

Sharp scissors

Glue (optional)

Felting mat

You can make lots of bees and you can scale them up or down. If you are using the amount for this bee to make life-size small bees, you should be able to make about 8 to 10 tiny bees

The honey bee is the larger of the bees shown here. The small bee is the alder cone bee. See p 78.

Body

1. Use the brown wool to make an oblong shape by rolling it into a tight sausage of approx. 8cm. Leave the wispy ends and stab your needle into those to secure the shape. Then stab all over to firm up the bee shape, making one end rounder (bottom), and the other a little more pointy (head).

2. When the shape is round and semi-firm, stab the needle into the centre to make an indentation so that the shape resembles a kidney bean shape but larger (7cm). It will bend in on itself.

3. Then take one third of the yellow (or a tiny wisp) and lay over the bee body approx. 1–2cm away from the more pointy front. Stab down. We don't want to give the bee a solid yellow stripe but more of a yellow dusting in the form of a softly edged stripe, so make sure you use very little yellow wool.

4. Then make another stripe 1–2cm further along and a final one again the same distance apart almost on its rounded end. The stripes do not have to meet on the underneath (this is where the bee curves up).

5. For a more anatomically correct shape, felt a groove just before the first yellow stripe which will distinguish the head from the body and with your fingers tease out a little wool at the back end of the bee to represent a pointy sting.

Wings

1. Tear off a very thin length (about 6cm) of the fine Merino top. Create a loop by folding in half. Hold the two ends together in your finger and felt the wispy ends in on one place in the centre of the first yellow strip but slightly on the side of the bee rather than on top. The wings should bend back towards the body. Repeat with the second wing.

2. If you want to make Angelina fibre wings, follow the instructions in the Techniques section (p 25). Once you have made the film, bend it in half and cut out two wings. Use a little wisp of yellow wool and lay it over the end of the wing whilst holding it against the bee's body, slightly sideways and pointing backwards. Secure the yellow wool

through the wing end into the body of the bee. Don't over stab as it will perforate the Angelina film. You can add a little glue, if you wish, by lifting the wing off slightly and putting a dab of glue underneath the wing towards the part that you have felted on. Make sure the wing is still sticking out from the side and from the top of the bee's body.

Alder cone bee

These little bees are so easy to make and involve no needle felting at all! The cones of the alder tree are easily found as they are the most common trees to be planted in town car parks. This is probably because they don't grow too tall when curtailed – this is also useful as you can pick the cones off the tree if there are none on the floor. I have found cones all year round as a lot stay on the tree but fresh ones are available from October. You can also identify the tree by the long catkins (which turn into the cones) and by the broad, round green leaves it has. The alder is the only British native broad-leaved tree to produce cones. You can of course scale the bees up by using larger cones from other trees too.

This project lends itself to letting little children make bees but also as a community/party project as the material costs are minimal and lots of people can get involved.

YOU WILL NEED

To make 10 alder cone bees

10 alder cones
1g yellow wool batts or tops
10 x 10cm greaseproof paper or white tissue paper
Hanging thread
Scissors

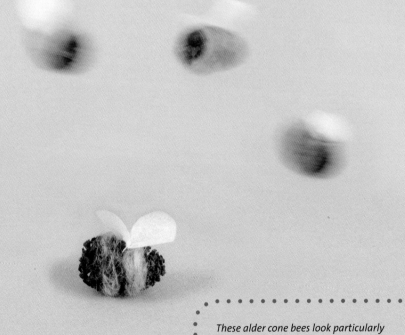

These alder cone bees look particularly effective in large numbers when hanging from a branch or tree.

Body

1. Use wisps of the yellow to wrap twice or three times around the cone, allowing the wool to sink slightly in between the scales.

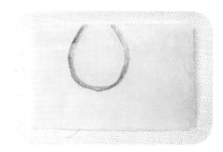 

Wings

1. Fold your paper in half. Then cut a semi-circle of about 1.5cm length out of the folded strip with the fold being the straight edge.

2. Once you have cut out your bee wing shape, unfold your paper and it should resemble a number '8'.

3. Now use your thread (about 20–30cm long) and wrap it once around the cone, making sure that it sinks right into the scales. You should end up with the two equally long ends and the cone hanging off it in the centre.

4. Position the paper wing so that its centre is between the two ends of thread. You will find that the wings are facing 45 degrees in the wrong direction but don't worry about that for now. Wrap the thread around the cone again, this time trapping the centre of the wing. And come up again so that the bee will hang fairly straight.

5. Secure your thread and then bend the paper wings in the right position, being careful not to tear them. It is OK if they are slightly crunched up where they attach to the cone. Your bee is finished.

Pocket mouse

Every child needs a pocket mouse! This may be the only rodent you will tolerate in your house and from experience I can share that my children took endless joy in pulling their mouse out of their pocket to scare others, usually grown-ups!

YOU WILL NEED

6g main colour wool batts, such as white Gotland, brown Country Sheep, grey South German Merino
1g flesh-pink New Zealand Merino wool batts
1g cream wool batts (only for the brown or grey mice, such as Fox Sheep, Cream South German Merino)
1 pair 4mm black glue-in eyes
12cm-long yarn in pink, beige or light brown
Coarse, medium and fine felting needle
Felting mat
Glue

The mouse measures 8–9cm nose to bottom (without tail)

Body

1. Using one of the main colours, take three-quarters of the wool and roll into a sausage shape with your fingers.

2. Felt the wispy ends down with your coarse felting needle so it holds its shape.

3. Then begin to shape one end round by stabbing the needle in semi-circles – this will be the bottom. Keep this part soft and round.

4. Taper the other by stabbing the needle from the centre of the sausage shape towards the end in a straight line and keep repeating from all sides. This will be the head.

5. Felt the whole shape down to a medium to hard felt. Make sure you keep turning the shape to keep it even. Your mouse will be about 8cm long without the tail.

6. If the shape appears too long during the shaping, stab your needle at a shallow angle repeatedly into the body lengthways. Decide which part is the tummy and which the back, and felt the tummy part flat so the mouse sits flat on the surface.

  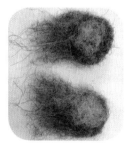  

Ears

1. Take two small pinches of the main wool colour (about 2.5cm round) and fold in half. Then fold the corners of each side next to the fold in and felt down with your medium needle. Remember to lift the ear off the mat regularly and felt it from both sides. This should make the top round while the bottom stays fluffy.

2. Add a wisp of pink on each ear on the inside only. You may have to tear off some of the wispy ends if they're too long before fastening onto the mouse.

Use the wispy ends by spreading them out and felt the ears onto the side of the head approximately ⅓ down the length of the mouse, slightly to the side.

3. Stab close to the ear then pinch the ears with two fingers whilst stabbing the needle all along the base of the ear. The more you stab around the base the more you can reduce the ear in size if necessary. At the very end stab into the inside of the ear to create the impression of an ear hole.

 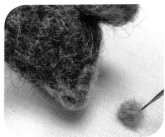  

Nose

1. For the nose, use a wisp of flesh-pink wool and colour in the front of the face with a very thin layer of pink like a dusting so that the main colour still shows through.

2. Then use a wisp of pink and pre-shape into a small ball by rolling it between your fingers. You may have to change to your fine needle now. Then secure with a few stabs on your felting mat before attaching it to the front of the face. It is best to stab around the edge of the nose rather than right through it to start with.

3. After the nose is fastened on, jab your needle repeatedly along the bottom of the nose to make a line where you imagine the mouth to be. Then stab the needle into the chin area to make the head more distinct from the rest of the body. Make a groove behind the ears with your medium or fine needle to mark the back of the head.

Eyes

1. Then make 'eye sockets' by felting an indentation on each side of the head where the eyes will go. The eyes should be in line with the ear hole, half way between the nose and ears.

2. Use your medium felting needle and make a hole from one eye socket to the other by sinking the needle into them until the handle sinks in. This will make a large enough hole to insert the pins of the glue-in eyes.

3. Check that they are symmetrical and add a tiny dab of glue behind them to fasten in. Leave to dry then add a tiny wisp of cream wool underneath the black eye (for the white mouse, use pink).

Tail

1. To make the tail, use one length of yarn and felt it onto the backside of the mouse. Then use a little of the main colour to cover the join.

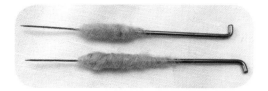

Legs

1. Make two front legs by using a pinch of flesh pink and split into two equal parts (for the front legs). Use another slightly larger pinch and split into two equal parts (for the hind legs).

2. Use your medium felting needle and wrap the wool tightly around it like a ribbon, keeping the wool flat and not allowing it to get twisted in the process. The two front legs should be 2.5cm long, and the hind legs 5cm. Slip the legs off the needle.

3. Felt the legs down with a couple of stabs to secure them but they should not need much felting if you have wrapped them round the needle tightly.

4. Next fasten the hind legs under the body towards the back and pointing backwards. Only felt 1cm of the leg onto the body. Felt from the legs onto the body facing forward.

5. Use some of the main coloured wool and cover the join of the hind legs including a little along the leg, just like a thin layer of fur. The pink will still shine through.

6. Attach the front legs. Use your fine needle and felt the front legs towards the tummy of the mouse facing forward but only fastening about half of the leg onto the body. The other half is not attached.

7. As before, use some of the main coloured wool and cover the join of the front legs onto the body.

8. Next take a wisp of the cream wool and felt onto the tummy like a dusting (you would not do this with the white mouse, but just keep it white or use a little pink for cover)

9. Bend the back legs forward so that about 2cm (or two-thirds) will be facing towards the head of the mouse now. Secure them down with the fine needle, mainly stabbing into the side of the leg into the body.

10. We want the legs to stay round and so need to fasten them on by stabbing around the shape rather than straight into them. The mouse should now sit comfortably resting on its legs.

11. As a finishing touch, add a groove by stabbing in a line with your medium or fine needle where you imagine the thigh and hip to be, as well as the elbow and shoulder, just for more definition.

Mermaid & Merboy

Mermaids and merboys have only become meaningful to me since I have had children and this has been mainly to do with the children's love of Rupert books! So, of course I had to create some from wool for them. I know there are many stylized versions. I prefer to keep mine simple but you can turn yours into characters inspired by stories you know.

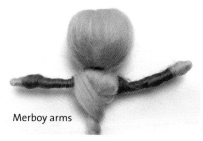

Merboy arms

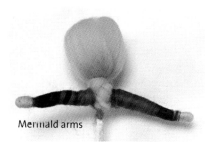

Mermaid arms

Head

1. Make the head according to the instructions on p 28, using most of the flesh-pink wool tops, just keeping some aside for the hands and all of the white wool batts.

Arms

1. Cut a 15cm length off the second pipe cleaner for the arms. Fasten onto the main pipe cleaner and wrap only the hands as outlined in the instructions for figures, on p 34.

2. Use the blue-green top for wrapping the rest of the arms on the merboy, and the pink-purple part of wool for the mermaid's arms.

Merboy

Mermaid

Tail and body

1. At the end of the main pipe cleaner, which has the head at the top, make a loop of about 5cm in diameter. Secure it by twisting the end around the main part and then bend it in so that it looks like a fish tail.

2. Now use your own blue–green mix of wool batts (for either your merboy or mermaid) and begin by wrapping the pipe cleaner body in a thin layer, winding the wool around as though it was a ribbon, keeping it flat rather allowing it to twist.

3. Open the pipe cleaner a little where the fish tail will be and wrap the pipe cleaner first before wrapping the whole tail. This will make needle felting it down later easier. Begin felting the wool down by using your coarse needle. Be careful not to stab too hard onto the wire of the pipe cleaner as this will bend or break your needle. Change to the medium needle if the wool gets too compacted to use the coarse needle.

4. Bend the mermaid or merboy where you imagine they would bend if they were to sit down and build up layers of wool to make a bottom.

5. If you are making a mermaid you may want to give her a more female shaping such as wider hips and a narrower waist. The merboy is more of a straight shape. Felt the wool down well, adding as you go along, then bend the arms up to felt under them

and also around the neck line. Your merboy/ mermaid should be able to sit. If not, add more wool to form a bottom. The Angelina fibre mixed into the wool will give the impression of water drops sparkling in the light.

Hair

There are different methods for adding hair to each figure:

1. The merboy uses a pinch of the multi-coloured wool batt (Dragon mix), which you lay over the head with plenty of wispy ends sticking out over the face area. Only felt on top of the head and down the back. Then use another pinch of wool of a similar size and lay it over the head so that the wispy ends hang over each side of the head. Again only felt on top of the head. Then use your scissors to trim first the front into a fringe and then around the sides so the hair is like a cap but so you can see the trimmed edges. Fasten on a little more to secure with your fine needle but not too much.

2. For the mermaid's hair, use a strand of curls and fasten them on around the face to frame it. Make sure the ringlets are hanging freely. Keep going around the head, adding strands of curls with a handful of ringlets hanging down.

Pom-pom hedgehog

Hedgehogs remind me a little of hogs as they have little piggy faces and make a loud grunting noise when foraging and eating, which is where they got their name from. Hedgehogs hibernate during the winter months and if you see one out and about it is a sign that he is either not well or that he is hungry. There are lots of local hedgehog rescue places and it may be best to take him to one of those. Did you know that a hedgehog has up to 5,000 spines and that they drop out after a year and then re-grow?

YOU WILL NEED

- 25g Jacobs brown stripy wool tops
- 15g caramel-coloured brown wool batts (I used Russian Karakul)
- Wisp of black wool batts (I used dyed New Zealand Merino)
- Pinch of dark brown wool batts (I used Portuguese Merino)
- Pair 4–5mm glue-in eyes
- Coarse, medium and fine felting needles
- Foam mat
- Glue
- 2 pieces cardboard, each 12 x 12cm
- Scissors
- 40cm strong thread or yarn
- Round dish of about 10cm diameter (or drawing compass)
- Round dish of about 4–5cm (or drawing compass)
- Pencil

The hedgehog measures 12–13cm long

Pom-pom spines

1. You will need two cardboard rings of the same size: about 10cm outer diameter and 5cm inner diameter. Cut an opening in both rings, which makes winding the wool as well as removing the card at the end easier.

2. Line up your two card rings so that the slits are aligned and wind the wool around them neatly, starting at the place where the cut has been made. Move slowly along, wrapping the card rings with the wool strand. When starting with a new strand of wool, continue winding in the same direction as this stops the layers underneath from getting unwound in the process.

3. When you have filled the cardboard rings, use sharp little scissors to cut around the outer edge. Once you have made a start you can slide the scissors between the two rings, which will make cutting easier. Cut all the way round, keeping your two rings in place. Your wound-up wool will stay on the rings as long as you are careful when cutting.

4. Now use about 40cm of the extra-strong thread and tie it as tightly as possible between the two cardboard rings. To tie a firm knot without an extra pair of hands see p 29. Cut the thread off with about 1cm remaining at both ends.

5. Finally pull the two cardboard rings off, making use of the cuts you made.

6. The next step is to cut a flat side into the pom-pom spines. Make sure not to cut too far into the pom-pom and accidentally cut the thread tied in the centre. Put this to one side.

Body and head

1. Use three-quarters of the caramel-coloured wool batts and roll into a sausage shape of about 8cm long. Hold the wispy ends down and felt them down with your medium or coarse needle so that it holds its own shape.

2. Stab all over to firm up and make one end round by stabbing in the end in a semi-circle from all directions. Make the opposite end pointy by stabbing the needle in a straight line starting from one third down the body's length towards the pointy end (the nose). Repeat and turn the shape continuously.

3. Next stab the needle from the front into the face area to build a forehead. You may have to repeat the shaping of the nose again and the shaping of the forehead until this part of the shape is the firmest part. The rest of the body should still be squishy and soft.

4. Now sit the flattened pom-pom on top of the hedgehog shape so that the head protrudes and the body is underneath. With your coarse felting needle begin to felt the body onto the pom-pom by stabbing into the sides of the hedgehog shape. Push hard and deep to fasten it but also to reduce the body size.

5. Alternate between fastening the sides onto the pom-pom and going all the way through the body. You are not felting the head. Change to a medium needle when the coarse one does not go into the wool easily any more.

6. Felt the hedgehog flat underneath so it sits without falling over.

7. Shape the head as before to create the domed forehead by stabbing straight into the face from the front and then readjust the pointy nose. Stop when there is no more give or your medium needle does not enter easily or when you have achieved the right proportions for the head and body. Turn the nose and head of your hedgehog up slightly by stabbing into the front from the underneath of the head, which will lift it up off the ground.

Face

1. Next use a wisp of your dark brown wool, split it in half and 'paint' the face of the hedgehog by laying each wisp from the tip of the nose to the imaginary eyes and felt it down.

2. It should be more like a dusting rather than a solid stripe, so keep the edges soft. Felt down with your medium or fine needle. Then add another wisp and cover the space in between the two others going along the bridge of the nose.

3. Make sure you keep this like a dusting too so that the whole feature is joined together but gives the impression of a thin layer rather than a dark patch.

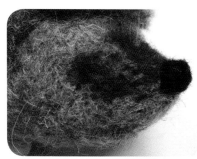

Nose

1. Take a wisp of black wool and roll it into a soft ball between your fingers. It should be about the size of a pea. Without pre-felting this, put it straight onto the tip of the hedgehog's face and secure it by stabbing your medium needle around the edges of the black, tucking it into place to make a black nose.

2. Initially it will look quite big but if you keep stabbing the needle around the edge, you will decrease the size and sculpt the nose directly onto the face. Whilst fastening and sculpting the nose you will have to also adjust the shape of the face and remember the nose should point upwards, so stab underneath the pointy end of the face too.

3. It helps to visualize the face if you make indentations for the eyes at this stage. Also readjust the forehead if necessary by pushing a needle straight into the face as you did earlier. The longer the nose part of the hedgehog, the older it will look. The stubbier, the younger and cuter.

Eyes

1. Use your coarse needle and insert this from one eye socket to the other all the way through the head until the wider part of the needle is inside. Move around a little. This will have created a large enough hole to insert the pins of the glue-in eyes.

2. Make sure they are symmetrical before adding a dab of glue behind the black pin (you need to pull the eye out again slightly) to secure. Leave them to dry.

Ears

1. Split a small pinch of the caramel-coloured wool into two equal parts. Fold one pinch in half and fold the corner in, where the folded edge is, felt down on your mat with your coarse needle. Then fold and felt in the other corner so you have a slightly pointy ear shape. Leave the wispy end on the opposite side un-felted.

2. The felted ear shape should measure about 2cm in length and 1.5cm in width plus the wispy ends. Pull off some of the wisps so that you only have about 1cm of loose fibres, which you will use to secure the ear onto the head. Make the other ear then fasten both on by spreading the wispy ends onto the side of the hedgehog's head, in line with the eyes, just in front of where the 'spikes' start and felt down.

3. Pinch the ear in with your fingers so that it creates a shell-like shape and felt down, concentrating around the sides of the ear. Adjust with a few stabs. If the ear appears too large, keep stabbing around the sides at the base, which will reduce the size.

To finish

1. Roll a tiny bit of dark brown wool between your fingers into a strand of about 2cm and felt into a mouth below the nose. Readjust the shape of the face and add a little more dark brown wool around the eyes if necessary.

2. Finally use your scissors and trim the pom-pom top if necessary. Do not cut unless you are certain, as we cannot add wool on again!

Autumn

· ·

Hairy spider

Mini apples & Apple girl

Toadstool

Toadstool boy

Mushroom

Leaves

Miniature pumpkins & Pumpkin girl

Snail

Acorns

Gnome

Pine cone gnome

Hairy spider

I am not a great fan of spiders myself, I admit, but can just about cope with these woolly ones. They are a great and really simple project to make and do not involve needle felting unless you want to add features (like a cross on the top or eyes). Make them in your preferred size and use them for a Halloween decoration if you like. You will be guaranteed to scare people with this realistic hairy spider!

YOU WILL NEED

2 x 30cm pipe cleaners (I used white extra-strong pipe cleaners)

5g black wool batts (I used dyed black New Zealand Merino but natural black Stonesheep works well too)

Pair small scissors or pliers to cut wire

Optional:

Foam mat

Medium and fine felting needle

The spider I made here measures about 6 x6cm.

This project is suitable for young children as you don't have to needle felt it.
Use black pipe cleaners so it will not matter if a little bit of pipe cleaner remains uncovered by wool.

1. Cut your pipe cleaner lengths into four 7–8cm pieces then fasten them together by twisting them around each other in the middle. Only twist them round once and make sure that you end up with similar length legs.

2. Tear off a pinch of the black wool, tease it into thin strands and start wrapping the wool about 1cm in from the end of one leg, out towards the end. Then bend the end over (to make a foot) and continue wrapping the wool up towards the body. Make sure your wrapping is tight so that the wool 'sticks' to itself and keep it flat like a ribbon (see Techniques p 21, for more details).

3. Wrap the end of the strand around the body, being mindful that each leg will have the ends of wool wrapped around the body so make sure you do not build up too much bulk. Tie the wispy ends of each strand tightly around the body so they fasten themselves into the wool or pipe cleaner. When each leg has been covered, bend the legs into shape.

Mini apples & Apple girl

YOU WILL NEED

For the mini apple

4g cream or white core wool batts (I use South German Merino, Shetland, Gotland)

Pinch of lichen green Mountain Sheep wool batts

Pinch of pale green New Zealand Merino wool batts

Wisp of salmon pink (I used plant-dyed New Zealand Merino)

Wisp of dark brown (Portuguese Merino)

Medium and fine felting needle

Felting mat

The apples are 5cm tall each, including the stalk.

Apples – not just a great symbol for British homegrown fruit but also a definite staple food in my family and we can never have enough in our house! My favourites are Discovery and Russet apples, though I sadly have to wait till August or September every year to enjoy them.

1. Roll the cream or white core wool into a ball with the wispy ends sticking out. Felt these down with your medium felting needle so that it holds its shape. Begin by shaping the apple as follows: stab your needle around the base to make it flat so it can stand. Then felt the lower part in so it becomes more narrow than the top part. Make an indentation at the top for the apple stalk. Keep stabbing the shape so it is nice and round towards the top and narrower towards the base.

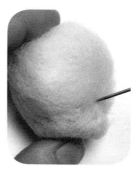

2. When the shape is firmed up and measures about 4cm diameter at the widest part, put to one side and begin mixing the greens together (refer to the Techniques section p 20). Take a slightly larger pinch of the pale green than of the lichen green, lay the two on top of each other and pull them apart, and continue layering like this.

3. Once you have a variegated green, lay a small quantity over the apple shape, felting this down with either your medium or fine needle, stabbing it from top to bottom and vice versa.

4. Continue until the apple is covered all around. You will end up with lighter and darker patches on the apple, just like a real fruit. If you run out of apple wool mix, make some more. Maintain the apple shape by stabbing the wispy ends into the top and bottom.

5. Once the apple has been covered in green, take a wisp of the green mix and add tiny wisps of the salmon pink into it. Add either only to a part of the apple or all over, depending how ripe you want it to look.

 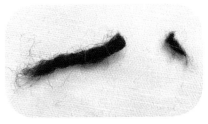 

Stalk

1. Take the brown wool and wrap it as tightly as you can around your fine felting needle, only covering about 2cm. Wrap it like a ribbon, meaning keep the wool flat, only making it as thick as the stalk should be. Slip it off your needle and give it a few stabs on your mat to secure but leave one end un-felted.

2. Then roll it between your fingers and cut the stalk straight at the end where you felted the shape down. The other end is still un-felted. Felt the stalk into place using your fine needle, stabbing the loose fibres into the apple. The stalk should reduce in size. If it is too long, trim another bit off.

If you want to add a leaf, follow instructions of how to make a leaf on p 107.

Apple girl

YOU WILL NEED

For the apple girl (about 9cm tall)

- 12g white wool batts (I use South German Merino, Shetland, Gotland)
- 3g light green wool batts (I use New Zealand Merino pale green)
- 3g darker green wool batts (I use Mountain Sheep lichen green)
- 1g dark red (I use New Zealand Merino dark red)
- 2g green, red, blue wool top (I used Australian Space dyed Merino 'flower garden')
- 30cm extra-strong pipe cleaner
- 2g flesh-pink wool top (I use South American Merino flesh pink)
- Strong thread
- Felting mat
- Coarse, medium and fine needles
- Pair of small scissors

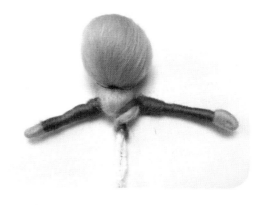

Body

1. Follow the instructions of how to make a head on p 28. Use 4g of white batts for the head.

2. Cut 15cm off the main pipe cleaner for arms (p 32) and use the flesh-pink wool tops just to cover the hands (p 33). Then wrap the green parts of the flower garden wool top around the arms. It's fine if a little blue or red shows – just make sure the dominant colour is green.

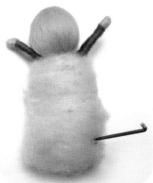

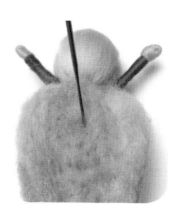

3. Build up bulk around the remainder of the pipe cleaner, bending it in a little at the bottom or even cutting a length off to keep within proportions.

4. Build layers of wool to reflect the shape of an apple, which is usually narrower at the bottom and broader at the top. Keep felting the layers down with your needle as you go and add more if needed. Bend the arms upwards to keep out of the way.

5. Next use your two green colours and mix them together (refer to the Techniques section p 20) by laying a good pinch of one colour on top of a good pinch of the other colour and tear it away between your thumb and index finger to give it a mottled or more variegated new colour.

6. Lay small amounts of the wool onto the white apple shape and felt it down from top to bottom. Repeat until it is fully covered. While doing this you can keep shaping the apple and make sure it has a flat bottom so it will stand. Felt all the way up right under the chin and around the arms.

7. Then take only a few wisps of the dark red and mix with a good pinch of the already mixed green and blend together the same way the greens have been mixed.

8. Lay wisps of the new mottled red-green onto the lower part of the apple and felt down from top to bottom. Repeat all around the apple base.

Hair

1. Take a 15cm-long strand of the green-red-blue wool top. Split it into three equal strands and plait. It is easiest if you pin one end into your felting mat with a felting needle as a stabiliser and then plait along to the end.

2. You can use another thin strand of the same wool to tie the ends off on both sides. Then cut the plaited strand in half.

3. Fasten the cut end against the head where you imagine the ears to be. Make use of the fibres coming open and spread them out so they are flat against the head. Repeat on the other side.

4. Take another smaller strand of the same wool and lay it over the top of the head with wispy ends hanging into the face. Felt the wool onto the bare parts of the head melting it in with the two plait ends. Don't worry about the variegation of red or blue coming through, as long the green is dominant. Finally, cut the wispy fringe and felt down appropriately to frame the face.

As an alternative, make an apple boy by felting wool onto the head, finishing off with a fringe.

Toadstool

When I was growing up my father would often take me into the forest to pick mushrooms. I always loved the colourful toadstools that grew alongside, although he taught me very early on that while pretty to look at, the toadstool is poisonous.

YOU WILL NEED

4g white core wool batts (I used South German Merino but white Shetland or Gotland will work too as well as Ryeland wool tops)

2g red wool batts (I used New Zealand Merino red)

Wisp of Cape Merino white

Medium and fine felting needles

Felting mat

This toadstool is 5cm tall.

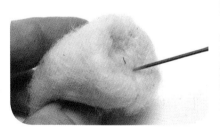

Stalk

1. Roll two-thirds of the white core wool into a sausage shape and felt down the wispy ends to secure the shape using your medium needle.

2. Then work on one end by stabbing straight into the end to create an indentation. This will help the toadstool to stand securely.

3. Felt the rest of the oblong shape by stabbing at a shallow angle from the top towards the bottom. This will firm it up but at the same time make the lower part more bulbous and the top more pointy.

Cap

1. Take all of the red and flatten into a circular piece. Use your medium needle and felt a central circular area of about 5cm. Only work on one side and keep lifting the wool up to stop it from fastening onto the mat.

2. Next fold the edges over in towards the flatter circular area, securing the wispy ends. Keep working on the same side. You will now have a round disc with thick, round edges.

3. Squeeze this shape down over your fingers and start stabbing on the inside, bending the edges down and round. This will create more of a cap and you can continue stabbing again underneath the cap to tidy the rough edges away.

4. Next fit the cap onto the stem. Using the remaining core wool, add a strand to the underneath of the toadstool, felting this into the red cap and the stem at the same time.

5. Make sure you do not stab the needle too far into the red when fastening the core wool to it, to avoid lighter fibres coming out on top of the cap. Work your way all around the underneath of the cap and the top of the stem until both shapes are securely fastened.

6. Then re-shape the red cap and top of the toadstool stem again. You are still using your medium needle.

Spots

1. Now roll 8 to 10 small balls from the Cape Merino between your fingers. They can be of varying sizes, and toadstools have sometimes small and larger spots all at once. Position each ball one at a time at the end of your fine needle and felt onto the top in random order.

2. Make sure you felt around the red once the white dot has been added, as you probably need to even out any indentations. Add more or fewer spots if you like.

3. A nice touch, if you have a little brown or green to hand, is to add a dusting around the base of the toadstool to give the impression of earth or grass.

Toadstool boy

YOU WILL NEED

- 15g cream wool batts (e.g. lanolin-rich organic South German Merino)
- 8g red wool batts (here New Zealand Merino red)
- 1g white Cape Merino wool batts
- 1g dark brown
- 30cm extra-strong pipe cleaner
- 2g flesh-pink wool top (I use South American Merino flesh pink)
- Strong thread
- Felting mat
- Coarse, medium and fine needles
- Sharp scissors

Toadstool boy is 12–13cm tall.

Body

1. Follow the instructions of how to make a head on p 28. Use 2–3g of the cream wool batts for the head.

2. Cut 15cm off the main pipe cleaner for arms (see p 32) and use the flesh-pink wool tops to cover the hands. Then wrap the cream wool batts around the arms, keeping it tight to create thin arms and teasing the wool apart as you go along.

3. Build up bulk with the cream-coloured wool around the remainder of the pipe cleaner, bending it in a little at the bottom or even cutting a length off to keep the proportions right (it should measure about 8cm from the bottom of the pipe cleaner to the neck). Build layers of the wool to reflect the shape of a toadstool stem, which is usually more rounded at the bottom and narrow at the top where the cap sits.

4. Continue felting the layers down with your medium or fine needle as you go and adding more wool if needed. Keep the arms up and out of the way. Once the bottom part is round enough, felt the underneath flat so the toadstool boy will be able to stand.

5. Add a little more wool around the upper arms and cover the join with wisps of the same wool to integrate back into the body.

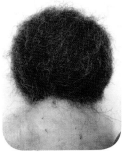

Hair

1. Felt a fringe with brown wool onto the head first by laying a strand of the wool over the face, then felt it down in a straight line almost from ear to ear on top of the head towards the forehead.

2. Cut the long strands off and felt the rest down over the top of the head. Then lay another strand of wool over the side of the head, felt down and cut off at neck length. Repeat on the other side and on the back of the head.

You should end up with a boy's bob hairstyle and a fringe at the front.

Cap

1. To make the cap, take three-quarters of the red and flatten it into a circular piece. Using your coarse needle, felt a central circular area of about 7–8cm. Only work on one side and keep lifting the wool up to stop it from fastening onto the mat.

2. Next fold the edges over in towards the flatter circular area and secure the wispy ends. You will now have a round disc with thick round edges measuring about 10cm in diameter.

3. Squeeze this shape down over your fingers and start stabbing on the inside, bending the edges down and round. This will create more of a cap and you can continue stabbing again underneath the cap to tidy the rough edges away.

4. Once you have a firm, tidy cap we need to fit it onto the head. Take a good pinch of the red wool and straighten it into a finger-wide length of about 15cm and felt it on your mat into a matted strand.

5. Then fit this inside the cap so that it forms a round nest shape that fits the head of the toadstool boy. Fasten this into the inside of the cap by stabbing mainly around the edges of the 'nest' shape.

6. Decide at which angle the cap should fit onto the head. Jab into the inner ring first by going all the way into the head and fastening the cap on like this in the first instance. This inner ring will almost disappear entirely and become part of the cap. Then jab the outside of the cap a few times, making sure that the cap is still in the right shape.

7. Next use the wisps of the cream wool to fill the inside of the cap with it, all the way around the hair. When adding the wool to the red inside rim, make sure you use your fine or medium needle and only stab superficially so that the cream fibres do not come out on the other side (the top of the cap). Adjust the shape of the cap again if necessary.

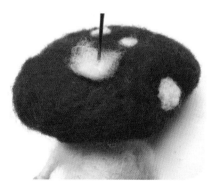

For a Toadstool girl, make plaits out of brown wool and felt to the head (see Apple girl, p 98).

Spots

1. Tear 10 to 12 small wisps from the Cape Merino. They can be of varying sizes, as toadstools can have small and larger spots. Position each wisp one at a time onto the top in random order, felting down as you go.

2. Make sure you felt around the red once the white dot has been added, as you probably need to even out any indentations.

Finishing touches

1. You could add any spare wisps or green or brown wool around the base of the toadstool stem for decoration, giving the impression of earth and grass.

2. You could also make a little toadstool for the boy to hold in his arms.

Mushroom

As a child my father would take me regularly to pick edible mushrooms. I always loved the variety of species and the delicate and delicious taste they had. I never once thought about the dangers of picking the wrong ones, as my father seemed to know what he was doing. I still love mushrooms and I am always up for trying the new flavours of more exotic species too.

YOU WILL NEED

30cm long extra-strong pipe cleaner
6g white core wool batt (I used South German Merino but white Shetland and Gotland will work too and so will Ryeland wool tops)
3g multi-coloured wool batts (I used New Zealand Dragon mix)
2g Country Sheep batts
4g Russian Karakul batts
Coarse and medium felting needles
Felting mat

This makes two mushrooms, the tallest being 5.5cm.

Frame

1. First of all you need to bend the pipe cleaner into a frame for the two mushrooms.

2. Make a loop at one end of about 4cm diameter and secure it by twisting the end around the long length of the pipe cleaner.

3. Bend the long end up into the centre of the loop .

4. Bend it back to make a 4cm tall stalk pointing up in the middle of your original loop.

5. Wrap the end of the pipe cleaner around the loop once and the end should now be about 6cm long. Bend the remaining pipe cleaner up to make a pin of about 3cm tall.

6. The two pins will be the stalks of the mushrooms, and the loop or circle will be the flat base of the slightly larger mushroom. It will also provide stability for the second slightly smaller mushroom next to it.

7. Now use your white core wool and, starting at the top of the larger pin, wrap the wool tightly around the pipe cleaner from top to bottom and around the loop until the wool runs out. Make sure you wrap the wool like a ribbon, keeping it flat and not twisting it. The wool should 'stick' to itself and as long as you wrap it tightly, you do not need to felt it down yet. If the strand tears or runs out, start with another, just making sure you wrap it in the same direction so that you don't unwrap the layers underneath. Then use a new strand and wrap the smaller pin, starting at the top and working your way to the connecting pipe cleaner all the way to the circular base of the other pin/stem.

8. Once you have built one layer with the core wool you can cover the whole base with the Dragon mix (coloured wool). Work in small batches and make sure that the base of the frame stays flat. Be extra careful with your needles as they can easily break if they hit the wire. You can either cover the bare minimum around the base of the mushrooms or spread the wool beyond the frame, felting it down flat on your mat. As long as the wire frame remains flat underneath, it should be stable enough.

Cap

1. Split the lighter brown into one third and two-thirds and do the same with the variegated brown. Mix the two-thirds of lighter brown with the two-thirds of variegated brown by laying them on top of each other and pulling them apart with your hands, then laying them on top again, and repeat a few times.

2. Then repeat with the one third and keep the two portions separate (small and large).

3. Start by making the smaller mushroom cap. Take all of the smaller brown mix and flatten into a circular piece. Use your medium needle and felt a central circular area inside of about 4cm. Only work on one side and keep lifting the wool up to stop it from fastening onto the mat.

4. Next fold the edges over, towards the flatter circular area, securing the wispy ends. Still only work from the same side. You will now have a round disc with thick round edges. Squeeze this shape down over your fingers and start stabbing on the inside, bending the edges down and round. This will create more of a cap and you can continue stabbing again underneath the cap to tidy the rough edges away.

 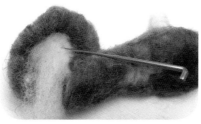

5. Next fit the cap onto the stem. Using the remaining core wool add a strand to the underneath of the mushroom, felting these into the brown cap and the stem at the same time.

6. Make sure you don't slab the needle too far into the brown mix when fastening the core wool to it, as we don't want those lighter fibres to come out on top of the cap.

7. Work your way all around the underneath of the cap and on top of the stem until both shapes are securely fastened. Then re-shape the brown cap and the top of the stem again. You are using your medium needle.

8. Make the larger mushroom cap and fix to the remaining stalk as for the small mushroom.

Leaves

YOU WILL NEED

Water soluble paper (15 x 15cm)

Wisps of New Zealand and Mountain Sheep wool batts of different colours but mostly oranges, yellows, reds, browns and greens

2g ready-mixed wool batts (New Zealand Dragon or Australian Merino Chameleon)

Felting mat

Coarse and medium felting needles

7-needle tool and brush mat (optional)

Pencil

Water spray bottle

The large leaf is 11cm long and 12cm wide.

As a child one of the compensations for the end of Summer was collecting the leaves that started to fall from the trees. I was amazed at how many different colours and shapes there were, and Autumn walks were slowed by my need to collect as many as possible. At home I would use them to decorate plates and make stencils, and now I collect them with my own children.

For this project it may be fun to collect your own leaves, which you can use to make a template. If you don't have any leaves use the template (right), or draw your own leaf free-hand or find a leaf image online.

1. Lay a piece of water-soluble paper just slightly larger than your leaf on top of your leaf or template. Make sure your leaf is completely dry as it only takes a drop of water to dissolve the paper. Using a pencil draw the leaf outline onto the water-soluble paper. Avoid using a felt tip pen or biro as the colours may run later when the paper gets dissolved.

2. Choose your wool for the leaf, and mix into the desired colours as necessary. To mix wool, take a pinch of two or more colours, lay them on top of each other and tear them apart with your thumb and index finger. Lay them of on top of each other again, tear again and repeat until the desired colour is achieved. Add other colours if you wish (see also Techniques, p 20).

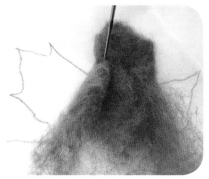

3. Lay a wisp of wool on the drawn motif on the water-soluble paper and begin to felt it, stabbing the needle into the wool.

4. Follow the pencil line as best you can with your needle and turn the wispy ends outside the line inside, finding the pencil line and felting them down. This will create a very neat line. Fill the leaf in by repeating this process.

5. It is always better to use small amounts of wool, thereby creating a thin felt and adding more if necessary, rather than using too much and not being able to take it off later.

6. When the whole leaf is filled in, hold it against the light and see if there are any weak spots that could turn into holes once the paper is dissolved. If needed, add more wisps of wool and felt them down. At this point a 7-needle tool and brush mat come in very handy They are a luxury rather than essential but I love the way they finish off the felting process by working seven times as fast!

Make lots of leaves and string them together or make a leaf mobile.

7. Next create some stringy wool ends by using a contrasting colour of green, brown, red or even yellow to felt in the leaf veins and a stalk.

8. Start by putting the stalk vein in first, then create little veins going off from the main one. It adds a little authentic detail to the leaf.

9. Using a spray bottle filled with plain water, spray the leaf a couple of times. Then squeeze the water into it until it saturates the whole leaf, though it should not be dripping wet. You will see the paper disappear quickly and should feel some sticky residue. This (invisible) residue will act like a fabric stiffener when dry and allows you to shape the leaf whilst wet so it remains that shape when dry.

10. Shape the leaf as you wish and put it inside a bowl or similar to maintain the desired shape while it dries. If you're in a rush you could put the leaves in a fan oven at no more than 60° Celsius/140° Fahrenheit or leave them on top of a radiator to dry more quickly. Once dry, your leaf will stay in the shape you dried it and it should feel stiff.

Miniature pumpkins & Pumpkin girl

Pumpkins are such a great project to practise needle felting, mixing colours and letting your creativity run free. My pumpkins are without faces or 'uncarved' but of course you can make your own variation. You can make them in all sizes too, life size or as mini decorations – or maybe as a doll's house accessory or even as play food! Remember pumpkins come in so many different colours too: bright red, oranges, yellow, white, greens, rusty brown and mottled mixtures of all of these colours.

To gauge the size of your pumpkin, take any amount of wool you like and roll it into a really tight ball. Once you have squeezed all the air out, it will give you an indication of the finished size.

YOU WILL NEED

For the miniature pumpkins

1g orange New Zealand Merino or Mountain Sheep wool batts; or ready-mixed New Zealand Merino batt Dragon or ready-mix Australian Merino wool batt Chameleon

Wisps of green, such as variegated green Mountain Sheep and New Zealand Merino

1 x small strand (2–3g) of dyed green Masham and/or Wensleydale natural brown curls or others such as Blue-faced Leicester

Felting mat

Coarse, medium and fine needles

The miniature pumpkins are 3–5cm tall and weigh just 2g.

Before you start, you can mix wool to get a more mottled effect or use a plain orange, if you wish. If mixing colours, lay the different colours on top of each other and pull them apart between your thumb and index finger. See the Technique section on p 20 for more details.

The fruit

1. Take the desired amount of the main wool and roll into a tight ball. Squeeze as much air out as possible. With a coarse needle felt down the wispy ends so it holds its own shape.

2. Then begin making your pumpkin shape. Pumpkins can be round like a football, sometimes oblong or they can be flatter like a squashed ball. Whichever shape, with pumpkins you can't go wrong!

3. Make sure you felt the pumpkin down nice and hard, which means continuously stabbing it all around, sinking the needle right into the centre each time. You may find that you have to use a medium needle to finish the shaping and firmness.

4. If the pumpkin is too small you can add more wool by applying layers of the main coloured wool over the pumpkin and felting these down so they 'melt' into the existing shape. Repeat this process if need be.

Stripes

1. Decide what colour the pumpkin stripes should be and how many to make. My pumpkins ended up with seven but I don't think there is a fixed number.

2. Make thin strands of the wool you decide to use for stripes. Just squeeze the wool between your thumb and index finger and roll it so it becomes string-like.

3. Lay one strand over the pumpkin from top to bottom and fix in at the top with your needle.

4. Then felt it in by stabbing in a precise line into the stringy wool all the way to the bottom, felting the end in or tearing some off if too much is left. If you run out of 'string', just add more and continue where you left it off.

5. You will notice that you are making a groove at the same time. That groove is typical for a pumpkin but you may have to readjust the shape of the pumpkin at the very end by felting all over again. Make sure stripes are evenly spaced.

Stalk

1. Take a small pinch of green wool and roll it between your fingers. Fold it in half. On your mat felt it into one solid stalk with wispy ends, then use one of these ends to fasten into the pumpkin top, right where all the stripes meet.

Curls

1. Felt a cut edge of the wool curl into the top next to the stalk, leaving the natural thinning end to hang by the side of the pumpkin. Pumpkins have curly 'tentacles' like vines and so this is very effective. If you wish to make leaves for a large pumpkin follow the instructions on how to make leaves (p 107). I have found that mini pumpkins don't need that level of detail.

Pumpkin girl

For the pumpkin girl

- 12g white wool batts (e.g. South German Merino, Shetland, Gotland, Fox Sheep)
- 1g orange wool tops (e.g. South American Merino 'Sunset')
- 4g orange wool batts (e.g. New Zealand muted orange or Mountain Sheep orange)
- 1g golden yellow wool batts (e.g. New Zealand Merino golden yellow)
- 1g green wool batts (e.g. New Zealand Merino mix variegated green or Mountain Sheep lichen green)
- 2g curls, either brown or green or even orange-yellow Wensleydale and Masham hand-dyed curls
- 30cm extra-strong pipe cleaner
- 2g flesh-pink wool top (I used South American Merino Flesh Pink)
- Strong thread
- Felting mat
- Coarse, medium and fine needles
- Sharp scissors

The figure is 9cm tall.

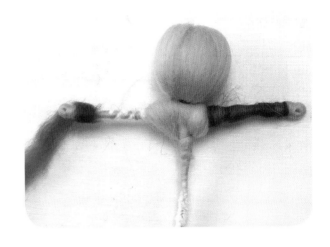

Body

1. Follow the instructions of how to make a head (p 28) using the materials listed left. Use 4g of the white or off-white wool batts for the head and keep the rest for later.

2. Cut 15cm off the main pipe cleaner for the arms (see p 32) and use the flesh-pink wool tops to cover the hands. Then wrap the red/orange top around the arms.

3. Build up some bulk with the white wool around the remainder of the pipe cleaner, bending it in a little at the bottom or even cutting a length off to keep the correct proportions.

4. Layer the wool to reflect the round shape of a pumpkin. Keep felting the layers down with your needle as you go.

5. Keep the arms bent upwards to keep them out of the way.

6. Now use your orange and yellow wool and mix small batches by taking a larger pinch of orange and a smaller one of yellow. Mix the wool as described in the technique section on p 20. Work in small batches if you are mixing the wool by hand. Combine all of the orange and yellow wool into a mottled or variegated new colour.

7. Add the coloured wool onto the white round shape by taking small quantities and laying it from the top down to the bottom, only covering small sections lengthways.

8. Felt this down with your medium needle, following the line when stabbing the needle from top to bottom.

9. Cover the whole shape all the way to the head, under the arms and over the top of the arms so that no white or flesh pink is visible any more.

10. Cover the bottom too and felt it flat so that the pumpkin girl can stand without toppling over.

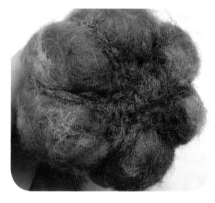

Stripes

1. Use the green wool and roll 7 or 8 strands between your finger about 10cm long (they need to reach all the way from the top to the bottom of the orange shape). Starting at the top, felt each strand down with a coarse needle. It will make an indentation, which is intentional.

2. The green strands will all join at the bottom and it will give you another opportunity to flatten this area so that the pumpkin girl will stand solidly.

3. Then use wisps of green and add them to the top of the pumpkin shape around the neck area.

Hair

1. Decide which is the best or smoothest part of the head and turn it to the front. You can turn the head by no more than 45 degrees. Lay one strand of curls over the head and start fastening them into the head. Concentrate on framing the face before covering the whole of the head.

Snail

Snails are not everyone's favourite, however children are fascinated by them. Perhaps it's because they can carry their own house on their back, or as in my case, because their eyes are at the end of the larger tentacles. The shells of snails can be very pretty and decorative, and therefore they have always featured on our seasonal tables.

This project is very simple and can be adapted so that an older child can have a go at needle felting, and a younger child could make the body of the snail (without tentacles) by using water and soap and rolling the wool into a sausage shape (wet felting).

YOU WILL NEED

2g multi-coloured wool batt (I used New Zealand Merino Dragon mix but you can mix your own – see the Techniques section, p 20)
1 snail shell (about 3 cm diameter, empty and cleaned)
Wisp of black wool top for eyes (optional)
Felting mat
Medium and fine needles
Glue

This makes one snail 5 – 6cm long.

Body

1. Roll 1g or half of the wool into a tight sausage shape, leaving the ends wispy. Felt these ends down with your medium needle so that the shape holds itself.

2. Then stab the needle all over to firm up the sausage. Concentrate the needle stabs on one end to make it slightly more pointy.

3. Stab the needle along the whole length of the sausage shape to make a flat 'stabiliser' or foot (see left) on each side.

4. Turn the snail over and felt a slight groove underneath the foot by stabbing the needle in a concentrated line along the body. This will make the snail lie flat.

Large tentacles

1. Next use your fine felting needle and a wisp of the main wool and wrap this around the centre of the needle no more than 1cm wide. Make sure you wrap it like a ribbon and keep it tight. Then slip it off.

2. Holding on to one end with your finger, give the small grain-like shape a few stabs with the fine needle to establish its shape.

3. Then fluff out the part you were holding onto and using those loose fibres, felt the shape onto the head of the snail to make eyes. Repeat with a second one.

Smaller tentacles

1. Felt down a wisp of wool into the shape of a wheat grain and fasten onto the head below the larger tentacles. Adding these features can be fiddly and you could leave the smaller tentacles out.

Shell fixing

1. Roll a ball between your fingers from a pinch of wool, making it the size of an olive. This shape needs to be able to fit inside the shell but make sure if you are trying it out, not to get it stuck!

2. Next use a small pinch of the wool to fold over the olive shape. Felt this on with your medium needle, leaving it open at one side.

3. Use these loose fibres to attach the ball to the top of your snail where you expect the shell to sit. Fasten it on firmly.

4. Try fitting the shell over the ball. Adjust the size by felting it down more or adding more wool so that it becomes a snug fit (you won't need to use glue unless you wish to).

5. Work on the size of the snail if the shell looks out of proportion. Stab your needle lengthways into the body to make it shorter. Add wool if you need to make it larger.

6. As a finishing touch, you could add a tiny wisp of black onto the tip of the larger tentacles for eyes. Use your fine needle and mind your fingers!

Acorns

There is something about the shape of an acorn that feels very satisfying and I am amazed at discovering how many different varieties of acorns there are when I had always assumed an oak tree is an oak tree. And yet the acorns that I find on the ground can be so different in size and shape. Hanging lots of these acorns on a Christmas tree or just having them around the house for decoration, maybe in a garland decorating the mantle piece, is lovely.

YOU WILL NEED

Wool batts – keeping to a theme, you could choose bright colours of the rainbow such as red, yellow, orange etc, New Zealand Merino or more natural browns and reds by using undyed wool batts, such as Russian Karakul, Fox Sheep, Karakul Honey, South German Merino, Karakul-Merino. You could also use muted variegated dyed colours, such as New Zealand mix batts variegated green, fox red, dormouse ochre

Medium and fine felting needles

Small felting mat

Acorn caps, dried

1–2g wool makes one life-size acorn.

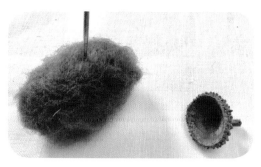

Nut

1. Take the desired (1–2g) amount of wool. If you are not sure how big the acorn will be, squeeze the air out of the wool by wrapping it tightly into a ball. You will see how small it becomes once the air is squeezed out.

2. Keep holding the shape tight without allowing it to pop open. You will have some wispy ends. Felt these wispy ends down with your coarse felting needle, so that the wool holds its own shape.

3. Now keep stabbing the needle all over to firm the acorn up and to keep shaping it into an oval. Watch your fingers and make sure you sink the needle right into the centre to needle felt the whole shape and not just the surface.

4. You will see that the fluffy fibres will disappear and the surface becomes more even. Keep stabbing and shaping into an even oval shape. Change to a fine needle if needed.

5. Try fitting the acorn into the cap and if it is too big, felt it down some more. If it is too round, you can roll it between your hands to make it more oblong and vice versa.

6. Once you have the desired size and firmness you can glue the acorn into the cap. A glue gun works the best but a good-quality fabric glue is good too.

Hanging acorn

1. If you would like a hanging acorn, thread a needle and make a knot into the doubled up thread. Push the needle through the inside of the cap all the way through to the knot. Make sure it does not slip through. Cut the thread off the needle and make a double knot at the end of the thread for hanging.

2. Glue inside the cap to secure the thread whilst pushing the acorn into place. Leave to dry before hanging your acorn up.

Gnome

My children have grown up with gnomes and *tomtens* (the Scandinavian version of gnomes). I have always liked the concept of a friendly little creature who watches over us at night and comes visiting our garden. My children used to leave out shelters and bits of food for them and used to be delighted to find it eaten in the morning or the remains of a tiny fire and sometimes even a little gemstone as a thank you.

YOU WILL NEED

15g white or cream core wool batts (e.g. Shetland, Gotland or South German Merino)

3g light beige wool batts (e.g. Fox Sheep)

12g natural brown wool batts such as Russian Karakul, Mountain Sheep (coat)

8g dyed wool batts for the hat, such as variegated green New Zealand and Stonelamb

3g dyed wool batts for boots (e.g. a New Zealand red)

3g curls in natural colours such as white, brown or grey

Wisps of dyed black New Zealand wool batts

Felting mat

Coarse and medium felting needles

This gnome is about 15cm tall with his hat on.

I suggest this gnome be kept safe as a decorative item rather than a toy as he is more delicate than some other projects.

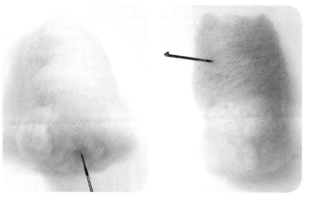

Body and head

1. Keep some wisps of the white wool core wool and taking the remainder, flatten it out with your hands into a sheet of about 18 x 18cm.

2. Fold the bottom edge up one third and then roll the whole thing into a cone shape with the folded part making the bottom of the cone (thicker end).

3. Felt down the wispy end first so that the wool is fastened.

4. Then stab your coarse needle all over to firm the shape up. The top of the cone needs to be round as this will become the head of the gnome. Stab the needle into the base to make it flat.

5. Once the cone is of a medium firmness, lay beige-coloured wool over the top half of the cone and felt down evenly. This is the skin colour of the gnome's face.

6. Keep a good pinch of the beige wool for the nose and ears.

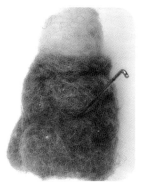

Coat

1. Use the natural brown wool batts for the coat. Keep about one quarter aside for later. Flatten the wool into a sheet on your felting mat and stab your needle so you are making a rectangular outline. Fold the wispy ends in and felt the whole shape down. Keep turning it to stop it from fastening onto the mat.

2. Once it is a fairly solid piece of felt, measure it against the gnome by wrapping him into it. The sheet should cover his body entirely and be a little longer, as well as close at the front. If it is too small, try and stretch it a little. If too big, felt it down some more or make it smaller as you felt it onto him.

3. Fasten it on with a few stabs around his body first. If you have a bare patch use some of the wool set aside to cover it but make sure you still have some left.

4. Now is a good time to make impressions of arms by felting two lines on each side of his body to make an arm. You can also make a collar by felting just below his neck around the coat.

5. Turn in the ends at the bottom and keep them soft and slightly wider to keep the impression of his coat dragging on the floor. Felt it down underneath him but keep the front of the coat open, as we will attach his boots here.

Boots

1. Use two equal parts of the red wool and flatten them into two similar-sized rectangular pieces of about 5 x 3cm each.

2. Fold each side into the centre lengthways, then turn by 90 degrees and fold only one side into the centre. Needle felt the thicker part into a rounded boot cap by stabbing it all over, leaving the rest wispy.

3. Now attach the wispy ends to the bottom of the gnome, checking that the boots stick out at the right angle and in the centre of the coat flaps.

4. Don't worry about it looking unsightly from the underneath, as we will cover all this up with the remaining brown wool at the end.

Little gnome footprints are easy to make using paint on the outside edge of your fist. Add toes with finger prints.

Nose

1. Roll a pinch of the light beige wool into a bean shape (size of a kidney bean) and felt down with your needle, keeping some wispy ends to attach to the face. Attach the nose with your needle by primarily stabbing the wispy ends first and then stabbing around the base of the nose rather than straight into it (this would flatten it).

Eyes

1. Make two indentations for eye sockets, each directly next to the top side of the nose.

2. Roll wisps of black wool into two peppercorn-size balls and felt into the sockets. Whilst you are working on the eyes, you may want to start shaping the rest of the face to firm it up a little. Stab around the side of the face to flatten it more and bring the cheekbones out. Don't worry too much about any facial expressions or a mouth, as most of the gnome's face will be covered with curls.

You can give your gnome rosy pink cheeks and colour his nose by using a pink-coloured powder blusher. Just apply a little where needed and blow on it to get the excess dust off. Add more blusher if needed, then blow any excess off again. Repeat until the desired colour is achieved.

3. Next take two tiny wisps of white and felt into the black eyeball for a reflection point. They should almost disappear into the eye and only just be visible.

4. Use wisps of the natural brown wool (reserved for the coat) and make tiny bushy eyebrows by felting wisps just over each eye.

Beard and hair

1. Use the curls to create a circular 'fringe' of curls all the way around the gnome's lower face and back of the head (neck).
Cut the curls into the right length before attaching them, as pulling them apart pulls the 'curliness' out of them.

2. Felt the cut ends down and leave the natural wispier ends hanging down. Keep the beard slightly longer than the hair.

Ears

1. Take two equal pinches of the beige wool and flatten them and fold them in the same way as the boots except on a much smaller scale (3 x 2cm before felted). The finished ears will measure about 2 x 1.5cm).

2. Attach them by felting the wispy ends down first. These should be laid out so they are facing towards the gnome's face.

3. Stab the needle in a concentrated spot at the base of the inner side of the ear to make an ear hole. Then give it a few stabs all around.

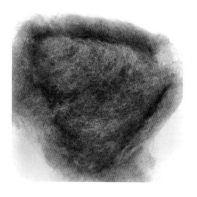

Hat

1. To make the hat, use your green-coloured wool and with your hands shape it roughly into a triangle, 12 x 12 x 12cm. Use your coarse needle and felt an outline of two straight lines and one outwardly curved line. The curved line will become the rim of the hat.

2. Fold the wispy edges in and felt all over to make a firm felted sheet. Make sure you keep lifting it off the mat and felt on both sides. Then fold the hat in half so that the straight sides line up and felt down through both sides to close the hat up.

3. Try to avoid making the join bulky by stabbing the needle close to the edges. We are not trying to create a really solid seam but just enough to fit the hat onto the gnome.

6. Strategic stabs all over will make sure it stays on his head. You can slightly stab into the side of the hat so that it looks as if it is slouching in on itself.

4. You can fit the hat so that the gnome's eyes are covered and just his nose is sticking out; you can show more of his face; or you can add some curls to the hat so they peep out from under his hat rim.

5. Fasten the hat on by stabbing the needle all over but not too much so that the hat looks 'glued' on.

7. The seam of the hat should now just be part of the hat at the back and barely noticeable. The ears will be sticking out from under the hat at each side.

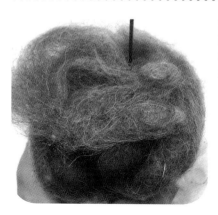

Finally use what you need from the brown coat wool to cover the base, making it look neat and allowing the gnome to stand solidly.

Pine cone gnome

This is an easier but very effective gnome that children can try with very few materials and easy techniques. You can make this gnome with or without legs.

YOU WILL NEED

A pine cone, preferably a little fat one
4g New Zealand Merino batt for the hat (I used red)
5g curls (e.g. Cotswold Lion curls)
1g of flesh-pink New Zealand Merino wool batt
Felting mat
Coarse and medium felting needles
Scissors, knitting needle or pencil
Glue (PVA glue, or use a glue gun)

Optional (to make legs):
30cm of extra-strong pipe cleaner
5g brown/grey wool batts (I used South German Merino)
5g dark brown wool batts (I used Milksheep)

The gnome without legs measures 13cm from the top of the hat to the bottom of the pine cone; with legs, 20cm.

Nose

1. Roll a small pinch of the flesh-pink wool batt into a tight ball, felting down the wispy ends first, then felt it all over to make it into a tight pear-shaped nose. If you are not making legs, sit your pine cone on the table and see which way it leans or whether it is stable at all. If it keeps falling over choose another one or cut the stalk off plus some more off the bottom to make it sit. Don't worry if it leans one way. Position the cone so it is leaning away from you.

2. Start by fitting the nose about one third down in between the scales. Don't glue it in yet as we are assembling the gnome first to make sure everything fits in the right place. For now just jam the nose in.

Beard

1. Use scissors, a knitting needle or a pencil and push the curls into the scales around the nose.

If you are crafting with young children, you could make the gnome's nose and hat and let the children 'dress' the pine cones.

Hat

1. Make the hat according to the instructions for the gnome in the previous project, then fit it on top. Your gnome should only show a big nose, as the hat reaches all the way down over his 'eyes' and the curly beard covers the rest of the pine cone.

2. To make the hat look slouchy or crumpled, stab your needle into the hat from the top whilst pushing the hat down with your fingers. Stab the needle a few times and the shape of the hat will change.

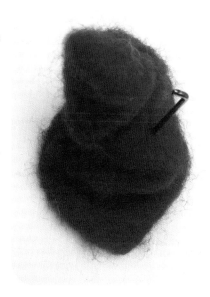

Once everything is in the right place, glue each part in bit by bit. Make sure you don't get glue onto the visible parts of the hat, beard or nose.

3. The hat is mainly fastened by putting glue into the scales at the back and pushing the hat into them.

4. Gently needle felt the hat to the nose using your medium needle. Once all is glued into place, leave to dry.

Legs and boots

1. If you are adding legs, wrap the brown grey wool around the pipe cleaner starting at one end. Make sure you wrap it like a ribbon rather than twisting it whilst wrapping it.

2. Bend the sharp wire end in on itself and cover the bend with wool. Keep the cover thinner around the middle of the pipe cleaner.

3. Repeat this starting from the other end. You should not have to felt it down as the wool you are using 'sticks' to itself like Velcro.

4. Use the brown and cover the ends of the pipe cleaner for 2cm. Bend it into a right angle and cover another 1cm with the same brown for the shaft of a boot. Needle felt the boot front down and into the top of the boot shaft.

5. Wrap the pipe cleaner around the lowest scales of the pine cone and let them 'dangle' down at the front. Making the gnome in this way will allow you to sit him on the edge of a shelf.

Winter

· · · · · · · · · · · · · · · · · · · ·

Donkey

Father Christmas

Snowman

Sheep and lamb

The Nativity: Mary, Joseph and Baby Jesus

Robin

Baubles

Christmas pudding bauble

Donkey

A few years ago we were approaching our house, returning from our summer holiday, and my husband said, 'I think I heard a donkey.' Our children and I soon heard the unmistakable '*eeeore*' ourselves. In our absence a donkey sanctuary had been set up across the valley from us with three donkeys in residence. I have always loved donkeys – their pretty faces and stubborn nature seem to capture the imagination. Our neighbours have become our morning alarm call as we can always rely on one of them to bellow between 5.30 and 6am regardless of the time of the year.

YOU WILL NEED

20g South German Merino brown grey wool batts
3g natural black Stonelamb wool batts (or dark brown wool batts or tops)
2g cream Fox Sheep wool batts
Wisps of white (Gotland, Shetland)
Wisps of black wool batts (I used natural black Stonelamb)
1 pair of 4 or 5mm black glue-in eyes
2 extra-strong pipe cleaners, 30cm long
Glue
Felting mat
Coarse, medium and fine felting needles
Scissors or pliers to cut the pipe cleaner
Scissors to cut wool

This donkey measures about 15–16cm in length.

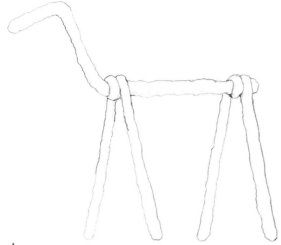

This is a more advanced project. I recommend you make some of the other projects in the book before you try this one.

Body

1. Begin by cutting one pipe cleaner in half (each one makes 2 legs 15cm long) and cut 16cm off the second pipe cleaner. Fasten one of the pipe cleaner legs around the longer pipe cleaner (16cm) approx. 7cm from one end.

2. Fasten it by twisting it around the pipe cleaner once. Make sure you have two legs the same length. Repeat with the second pipe cleaner at the end.

3. Separate a finger width of wool from your main wool (brown/grey) and tear off so you end up with a strand. Begin wrapping thin layers around one foot 5mm into the pipe cleaner. Cover about 1cm then bend the pipe cleaner back about 6mm so that the bent part will be covered in wool and continue wrapping the pipe cleaner to cover the sharp end of the pipe cleaner.

4. Remember to wrap the wool like a ribbon, which means not twisting the strand of wool (see Techniques section, p 21). Bend the rest of the frame out of the way to help you wind the wool around the leg.

5. Continue all the way up, then wrap the remainder of the strand around the body. If your strand tears, fasten it on again by using the wispy ends to secure the strand and continue wrapping in the same direction as before (this is important so you do not unwrap the layers underneath).

6. As you are using a wool batt to wrap the frame, you have to gently tease the strand as you go along, making sure you keep the wrap thin and tight. Build more bulk around the body. Repeat with the other three legs.

7. Use another strand and begin wrapping the whole of the long pipe cleaner starting at the head. As with the feet, bend the end of the pipe cleaner in to cover the bend and hide the sharp end. Begin to imagine the shape of the donkey you are aiming to make. Build up more wool and bulk by wrapping thin layers onto the head and body and less for the neck. Be sure to keep the layers thin and tight. At this stage you do not need to needle felt the wool down.

8. Next use your medium needle and begin to felt the wool down so that all the loose areas are firmed up. Make sure you avoid the pipe cleaner and be careful not to bend or break your needle on the wire. Felting the wool down will give you a better idea where you need to build more bulk by wrapping more wool around the frame. Make sure you give the donkey a straight back.

9. Next build the legs up to be more in proportion with the animal. Wrap more wool around them, starting from the foot. Wind the rest of the strand around the shoulders or bottom to help build up bulk. Felt down each time you finish a strand of wool. Do not be afraid to pull the whole figure into shape with your fingers by pulling on a leg or twisting parts into place. Add bulk around the bottom, chest and head.

10. You may want to lay small patches of wool over the part you are trying to make bigger and stop wrapping the wool now, but add wool with more of a focus where it is needed and felt it down with your medium needle. Use wisps of wool to cover cracks and joins.

11. To give the donkey more of a prominent bottom, pull wool you have wrapped around his backside down over his bottom and felt it down. It is like 'putting meat on the bone', so keep adding wool. If it looks too bulky, either take it off or felt it down. You should have a lot of air in the shape still. If the legs are too bulky, stab your needle at a shallow angle along the leg from the foot upwards towards or even into the body.

12. Pay particular attention to the following features: donkeys have large tummies, so make sure to build up bulk there. They also have broad bottoms. The line from the top of the head going across the neck and to the bottom is straight, especially when their head is slightly bowed. They have strong jaws and so make sure to add wool to the side of their faces to reflect that. Make sure to add wool to their chests too!

13. Make a groove with your needle from the groin area going up to show off the thigh muscles and hips. Do the same for the front legs, making a groove by starting under the 'arm' following the line up to the shoulder blade. You make a groove by stabbing your needle in a line over and over.

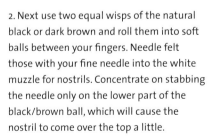

Muzzle

1. Take a wisp of the cream wool and wrap around the muzzle. Felt it down so that the line between the white and grey stays soft.

2. Next use two equal wisps of the natural black or dark brown and roll them into soft balls between your fingers. Needle felt those with your fine needle into the white muzzle for nostrils. Concentrate on stabbing the needle only on the lower part of the black/brown ball, which will cause the nostril to come over the top a little.

3. Enhance this feature by adding a tiny rice-size piece of off-white wool over the top to give the impression of a slight 'overhang'.

4. Next use a small strand of black/brown wool and needle felt again with your fine needle into a mouth.

Eyes

1. By now you will have a good idea by looking at the donkey's face where the eyes are going to be. Make two symmetrical indentations with your medium or fine needle for eye sockets.

2. Fill those with the white (cream) wool. Next use your medium needle and insert it into the centre of one white patch all the way through the head, coming out at the second white patch. Push the needle through so that the handle has gone into the wool. This will make a large hole in both eyes.

3. Pull the needle out and insert the glue-in eyes. If you are happy with the position, pull the eye out a tiny bit and add a little dab of glue. Push back in and leave to dry.

Ears

1. Take the brown grey wool you set aside earlier and split it into two equal parts. With your coarse needle, 'draw' an outline of an ear onto the wool by stabbing the needle in a line. Fold the wispy sides in, leaving the end fluffy (where the ear will attach) and felt down more. Make sure you lift the wool regularly off the mat so it does not get fastened to it. Felt on both sides. Keep folding the sides over until the ear measures about 2cm across the widest part

and 5cm in length. Stabbing the needle at a shallow angle only into the wool will reduce the size of the ear and stop the fibres from going too far into the felting mat.

2. Next add a little black wool for dusting around the edges and another dusting of cream wool on the inside. When fastening the cream wool, allow the ear to curve inwards as you are stabbing the needle in the centre.

3. Tear excess wisps off at the end of the ear if it is longer than 5cm. Lay the ear onto the head, face up, leaning back towards the body. Felt some of the wisps down before standing the ear and checking that the positioning is correct. Then pinch the ear at the bottom with one hand and felt it on to the head, slightly curved inward.

4. Felt all around the base and adjust the shaping of the head if necessary.

Hooves

1. Use the black/brown wool and wrap the end of the foot tightly. Felt down with your fine needle. Felt from the bottom as well to make it flat.

2. Mind your needle as it can break easily. It may be easier to felt sideways into the foot at a shallow angle rather than straight into it. Repeat for all four feet.

Cross and mane

1. With the same wool, needle felt a line on the back of the donkey all along the spine. Using the same wool, make another line across the shoulder, crossing the spine line and ending on top of the leg/shoulder.

2. Next, using the black or brown wool, lay a patch of wool of about 9–10cm in length and 3–4cm wide along the head from between the ears, and felt down in the centre lengthways following the spine.

3. When it is fastened on, pull the fibres up and trim with scissors into a brush.

Tail

1. For the tail, still using the black/brown wool, take a pinch about 6cm long and roll it between your fingers so only two-thirds of it makes a string, leaving the rest fluffy. Felt the string part down with your medium or coarse felting needle on the mat.

Finishing touches

1. Use the the black/brown wool and add tiny wisps on the top of the eyes for eye lashes.

2. Using the cream wool, give the donkey a dusting on his tummy. Take this opportunity to tweak the shape here and there.

Father Christmas

Being German I have always found the figure of Father Christmas confusing. In Germany we celebrate Saint Niklas (Nikolaus) on 6 December and the story has it that he was a bishop and saint. He is also known as Father Christmas, Santa Claus and many other names depending on the county and culture we live in.

In German households it is the Christ Child (Christkind) that delivers the gifts on Christmas Eve and the image of Father Christmas coming down the chimney has always been a thing I only saw on TV as a child. I found out later as an adult that in fact the benevolent and kind gentleman dressed in red has many guises and names and appears in many places around the world at different times of the year!

YOU WILL NEED

8g flesh-pink New Zealand Merino wool batts

20g white wool batts (e.g. South German Merino, Shetland, Gotland, Fox Sheep)

25g red New Zealand Merino wool batts

5g white Cape Merino wool batts

5g Mohair tops or use other curls such as Masham or Cotswold Lion curls

1g dark brown or black wool batts or tops (I used dyed New Zealand Merino wool batts)

1 pair of 4–5mm glue-in eyes

3 x 30cm pipe cleaner

Strong thread

Coarse, medium and fine felting needles

Felting mat

Sharp scissors

Scissors or pliers to cut the pipe cleaner wire

For Father Christmas's sack
2 pieces of hessian, each 12 x 13cm
A darning needle
Strong yarn
Any kind of wool batt (to fill the sack)

This figure is 20cm tall.

Head

1. Use about three-quarters of the flesh-pink wool batts, about 25 x 10cm in size. Try to allow the direction of the fibres to run lengthways. Keep the rest for wrapping the hands.

2. Bend a pipe cleaner end in on itself about 3cm down from the top. Hook the pipe cleaner onto the middle of the strand of pink wool and secure it by twisting the end of the pipe cleaner around the long end.

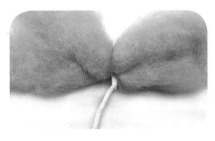

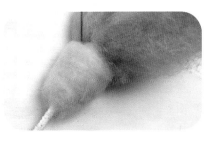

3. The wool top should be fastened securely. It will look a little like a moustache.

4. Move the pink wool out of the way by bending it up away from the pipe cleaner.

5. Start wrapping the white wool batts around the top of the pipe cleaner just below the pink 'moustache'. Wrap it flat like a ribbon, letting go of the end once a full round has been completed.

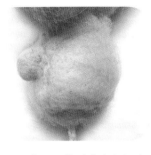

6. Build the layers up slowly and felt them down with your medium needle as you go, until the head is ball shaped and measures about 5cm. Choose a side of the white ball that looks nice and even: this will become the face.

7. Roll a pinch of the white wool between your fingers and felt down on your mat until it holds its own shape. This is the nose. Attach the nose onto the face by stabbing the needle into the edge of the nose where it meets the face.

8. Make sure the needle sinks into both the edge of the nose and the face. Don't stab the needle straight into the ball as you will lose the round shape.

Add more layers if the nose is too small, but it is OK for it to look slightly too large.

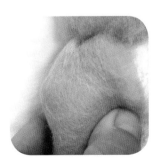

9. Next pull a thin layer of the flesh-pink wool tight down over the face to see how the nose looks. Add more wool to the nose or pull less flesh-pink wool over the face as needed.

Once you are happy, pull the remaining flesh-pink wool over the rest of the head and tie the head tightly at the neck using a strong thread.

10. To tie the thread, feed the thread round the first knot twice instead of once (see p 29). This will stop the thread from slipping open when you need to let go of it in order to make the second loop. This way you can tie the neck really firmly without the help of a second pair of hands.

11. Next felt around the now pink nose by stabbing in and around it and make two indentations for the eyes on either side by repeatedly stabbing the needle in one spot.

If despite your efforts, white wool from underneath shows through, don't worry. Our Father Christmas will not show much of his face as he will have a moustache and beard.

Arms

1. To make the arms (see p 32), take a new pipe cleaner and wrap it around the main pipe cleaner once so that two same-length arms are sticking out horizontally. Push the arms up so they are positioned just below the head.

2. Next move the flesh pink that is left hanging below the tie out of the way. Wind that wool around and down the central pipe cleaner, and felt it down.

Hands

1. Use the flesh-pink wool and wrap a very thin layer onto the end of the arm pipe cleaner, covering only about 6cm. Make a fist as follows: Bend 1cm of the wrapped pipe cleaner back on itself, then bend 1cm in the opposite direction. This makes a thumb (see above).

2. Repeat this process by bending the pipe cleaner end back on itself into a larger loop, which makes mitten fingers (see above).

3. Fasten the loose end onto the arm by wrapping a thin strand of flesh-pink wool tightly around the wrist area (see above).

4. Wrap flesh-pink wool around the hand area so that you end up with a mitten-like hand. Felt down as you go but be careful of the wire!

Finishing the arms

1. Cover both arms all the way up with layers of the flesh-pink wool until they are about 1cm thick.

Body

1. You now need to extend the main body pipe cleaner to make a circular base for the figure. Attach a new the pipe cleaner to the main body by twisting the two together, starting as high up as possible below the felted body. Make a loop at the end of the pipe cleaner extension and bend it to sit at 90 degrees and form a round base for your figure to stand on.

2. I suggest that your Father Christmas should be no taller than 20cm as the pipe cleaner (even though they are extra-strong) will not be able to support his weight otherwise.

3. Use some more of the white/cream wool and wrap the full length of body pipe cleaner all the way to the loop at the bottom but not around the loop. Build up a layer of about 4–5cm in diameter and felt it down. This will also help the pipe cleaner join to become more solid.

Cloak

1. Take most of the red wool, leaving about 10g for the hat and for patching up later if necessary.

2. Flatten the red wool into a 30 x 20cm rectangle and make a hole in the middle.

3. You can felt the whole flat shape down a little to ensure it holds together. To do this, stab your needle at a shallow angle into the red wool and make sure you lift it off the mat regularly so it doesn't fasten onto it.

4. Put the cloak on over Father Christmas's head. The cloak should reach all the way to the wrists and beyond the bottom loop of the pipe cleaner.

5. Felt a solid seam under the arm by stabbing your medium or coarse needle in a straight line all the way from the hand to the armpit. Make sure that the hand is fully exposed and that the seam allows for a loose fit of the sleeve. The arm, including the sleeve, should measure 3cm in width.

6. Felt this seam line from both sides on both arms. Once you have a solidly felted line, use your scissors and cut below the arm and just below the felted seam. The sleeve should stay closed.

7. Pull the sides of the red cloak open below the arm. Starting at one side, tuck one part in towards the front under the red cover and then bring the other end onto the back. This will tidy away the sides but also build more bulk on the body. Repeat on the other side and felt both ends down on the back.

8. If need be, use a little red to cover the area at the back where the two side flaps have been felted down in case of unevenness.

Double check the arms by bending them upwards and felt down any weak areas in the seam.

9. Straighten the cloak by pulling it gently downwards and tuck it under the flat base loop.

10. Use your cream/white wool to stuff the inside of the shell of the cloak, making sure you do not tear it in the process.

11. Then felt the whole figure down from the outside into the red wool to make the red cloak more solid and shapely. Use more red wool to cover up uneven patches and close the bottom by covering with red. Make sure that the pipe cleaner is totally hidden.

Hat

1. Use about 5g of red wool and with your hands shape it roughly into a triangle, 12 x 12 x 12cm. Use your coarse needle and felt an outline of two straight lines and one outwardly curved line. The curved line will become the rim of the hat (see the Gnome's hat on p 122).

2. Fold the wispy edges in and felt all over to make a firm felted sheet. Make sure you keep lifting it off the mat and felt it from both sides. Then fold the hat in half so that the straight sides line up and felt down through both sides to close the hat up. Make the join as smooth as possible by stabbing the needle close to the edges.

3. We are not trying to create a really solid seam but just enough to fit the hat onto the head. You could start by using your coarse needle to secure it and then your fine needle to finish it off. Put the hat to one side and continue on the details and face.

Eyes

1. Fill the eye sockets with just a few wisps of the white Cape Merino.

2. Then poke your felting needle into the centre of the eye by sinking it all the way to the thicker round part so that it makes a hole for the glue-in eyes. Insert one eye and repeat on the other side. Make sure the eyes are in the right position, then pull out a little, add a dab of glue and push them back in and leave to dry.

3. Roll a tiny wisp of the dark brown into a thin thread between your fingers. Fasten this onto the outside of the white like an eyeliner. Felt on as you go along.

Nostrils

1. Next make two holes for nostrils with your medium felting needle by stabbing the needle repeatedly into each place.

Cloak fur trim

1. Next use the Cape Merino wool and add the fur trimmings to Father Christmas's coat.

2. This wool is ideal for giving a fluffy and white finish and only needs to be stabbed in place with a fine needle. You can do this as you go along. Start with the sleeves and make sure to stab the white inside the opening of the sleeve to hide all red.

3. Then create a white line from the top of the collar all the way to the floor, curving slightly towards the bottom as though the coat is open there. Repeat on the other side. Make a white trim all around the base back and front.

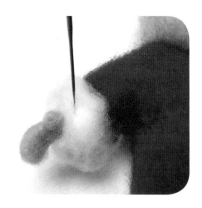

Beard and hair

1. I made my own curls for Father Christmas's beard and hair by crocheting 1cm-thick strands of Mohair tops with a 4mm crochet hook. You can read how to make curls in the Techniques section (p 22). You could use the Mohair uncurled. It is actually hair from a goat and is not classed as wool.

2. Start with the beard. Choose a strand of curls and fasten them on.

3. I used one long strand and zig-zagged it along the chin, turning back when the beard length was achieved. You can use several shorter strands of curls or straight wool/hair. We want his face to be framed by the hair. Only cover the parts that will be visible when the hat is in place.

4. Try the hat on to see which parts can be left bare.

Finishing the hat

1. When you're happy, fasten the hat on by stabbing into the rim and head with a medium felting needle. If there are any bare red patches, cover with a wisp of red. My Father Christmas wears his hat over the forehead and his hair is almost covering his eyes so he does not need any more facial features, such as eyebrows.

2. Using the Cape Merino wool and a fine needle, add the fur trim around the edge of the hat.

3. If you want his hat to be slouched and hanging down at the back, place it into shape with your fingers and stab the needle a few times into the hat so that it stays in that position.

4. Finally roll a soft ball of the white 'fur' wool and fasten to the end of his hat for a bobble. As an optional extra, use some blusher and a cotton bud and give Father Christmas rosy cheeks and a rosy nose.

Sack

1. Lay your two pieces of hessian on top of each other. Using strong yarn, sew around three sides with a back stitch about 1cm away from the edge. Then turn the sack inside out.

2. Use the same yarn to make a tie at the top by making a running stitch along the open edge of the bag, 1cm in from the cut edge.

3. Fill with wool so it looks full and tie the yarn together. Secure with a knot and use the end of the yarn to fasten onto Father Christmas's hand, either to have the sack over his back or to hold by his side.

Snowman

I love snow, lots of it, over a prolonged period of time. I love that feeling of cleanliness and wading through white snow and your shoes becoming cleaner than ever. I love the sound of the crunching under my feet, even the idea of being snowed in when everything comes to a standstill for a precious moment, and I love watching the children play in this great magic white stuff! I miss snowy winters and perhaps that is why I feel there should be a snowman in this book!

YOU WILL NEED

25g white core wool batts (I used Shetland)
5g Cape Merino wool batts
Pinch of orange wool batts (I used Mountain Sheep orange)
Pinch of black wool batts (I used Stonelamb natural black but New Zealand Merino dyed black works well)
1 pair of glue-in eyes 6 or 7mm
2g coloured wool batts (I used New Zealand Merino Dragon mix, for the hat)
Finger-width coloured top, a minimum of 30cm (I used Australian Merino Sunset)
Coarse, medium and fine felting needles
Felting mat
Glue
Small sharp scissors

The snowman is about 18cm tall, including his hat.

Body

1. Take two-thirds of the white core wool and roll into a soft oblong shape, felting down the wispy ends at the end to secure the shape using the coarse needle. Then make one end into a flat bottom and keep the top rounded. Felt it all over to make it a little firmer but keep the shape quite soft. It will look more like a cone now.

2. Next use two-thirds of the remaining white core wool and roll it into a ball for the head, again felting the wispy ends down to secure the shape. Firm this shape up by stabbing it all over and making sure it is nice and round, like a snowball.

3. Then tease the wool on the top of the cone shape apart, making a crater. Fit the round head inside and felt down the teased-out fibres of the cone into the head to felt it onto the cone shape.

4. Work on the neck until the head is securely fastened and the snowman now has a neck. Use any of the spare white if you need to add wool.

5. Next cover the whole shape with a thin layer of the very soft and fluffy Cape Merino so it looks like a fresh snow fall. Use your medium or fine needle for this.

Nose

1. Flatten out your orange wool. Then fold it in half; the straight fold becomes the point of the carrot nose, so roll it up accordingly, then felt down with your medium needle into a cone shape, keeping the ends wispy.

2. Roll the cone between your fingers to flatten down any fluffy bits. You may also have to shorten the cone end as we don't want an orange mask. Just tear wisps off without distorting the felted carrot shape.

3. Then fasten the nose on by stabbing the wispy orange fibres into the white right next to the carrot shape. If you have too large an area of orange showing, use a little of the Cape Merino and cover it up again.

Eyes

1. Make two holes with your felting needle for the eyes, close to the nose, pushing your needle into the wool all the way, wiggling it about a bit without breaking it and pulling it out again.

2. You should now be able to insert the pin of the eye. Fit both eyes, making sure they are in the right place before you add a dab of glue behind them to fasten them in.

Facial features

1. Take a wisp of the black wool and tease it into a thin strand. Roll this between your fingers to make it more string like. Cut two eyebrows and a length for a mouth with scissors.

2. Lay them out on the snowman's face and play with his expressions by changing the features around.

3. Decide which expression works for you, then felt down with your fine or medium needle. Reshape the face again a little – it may have gone out of shape whilst attaching the mouth and eyebrows.

Scarf

1. Add the scarf by wrapping the orange wool top around his neck and tie it once. I cut the wispy ends straight so it looks more like a scarf. Secure the knot by felting it into the neck with a few stabs with your medium or fine needle.

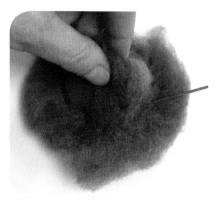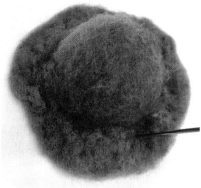

Hat

1. Flatten your coloured wool batt into a circular shape and felt with your coarse or medium needle into a circle of approx. 6cm. At the same time, tease the wool inside the circle upwards but don't tear it, just pull it up so it forms a dome.

2. Keep lifting the hat off the mat so it does not get fastened onto it. Then fold the wispy ends in towards the edge of the dome to make a brim. The dome part stays un-felted.

3. Once you are happy with the shape, decide at which angle it should be worn and felt it down only along the edge of the dome. Leave the brim free and do not felt the dome down either.

Extra features

1. You could add buttons down the front of your snowman, or you could put a small stick (twig) on each side of his body. Just make a hole with your felting needle or perhaps a larger pin and insert twigs, securing them with a dab of glue.

2. You can also give your snowman an impression of arms and legs by using your coarse needle and making an indentation on each side for the arms and indentations down the bottom half for legs. It's better to do this before you add the scarf and buttons.

Sheep and lamb

If it wasn't for sheep, this book would not exist! Over the past years I have become to truly appreciate the enormous versatility of wool and am fascinated by the variety of colour and texture the different breeds can produce. Wool is not just used for clothing, carpet and making decorative items. It is also more and more popular for insulation.

The sheep here are made in a very simple way, and they go very well with the nativity scene but are also great for decoration all year round, especially with their lambs.

The materials and instructions are shown for an adult sheep. Information for making the lamb are included in brackets throughout the instructions.

YOU WILL NEED

8g white wool batts (lamb, 5g) (I used the South German Merino and Ryeland Lamb)

3g Leicester curls (they are particularly tiny and therefore suitable for making small sheep)

Wisp of brown wool batts (I used Portuguese Merino)

Wisp of flesh-pink wool batts (I used New Zealand Merino)

Medium and fine felting needles

Felting mat

The sheep is 10cm long, the lamb about 7cm long.

Body

1. Use half of the main white wool and roll into a tight sausage with your hands. Then felt the wispy ends down with your medium needle into the rolled-up shape so that it will hold together. Then needle felt all over to make an oblong shape with two round ends.

Head

1. Take half of the remaining white wool and flatten it out into a rectangle. Fold this in by one third lengthways and then roll it up width-ways. You should end up with a bulkier end (where we did the first fold), which will become the face and mouth of the sheep.

2. The wispy ends will be used to fasten the head onto the body. Felt the head shape down with your medium needle. Sheep heads are quite broad and the face is fairly long (for the lamb, make the shape of the head stubbier). See how the head fits onto the body in terms of size and proportions.

3. If necessary, tear off excess wisps. Hold the head onto the body with the wisps spread all around and felt down with your medium needle, making it into one shape. Stab your needle straight into the face area at a shallow angle to shape the muzzle and make a domed forehead.

Ears

1. To make the ears (the ears for the lamb are the same size as for an adult sheep), tear off two equal-sized pinches of the white wool and needle felt each separately on your mat by folding the wispy ends in but leaving some at the end to allow the ears to be fastened onto the side of the head. The shape of the ear is like a leaf.

2. Add a little pink on one side of each ear. The finished ear so far measures about 2cm without taking the wisps into account. Make the other ear. Now position both symmetrically on each side of the sheep's head so that they stick out at right angles.

3. Spread out the wispy ends before felting them down to secure them and pinch them at the base so that they fold inwards, creating the impression of an ear hole, and felt into that place several times. Look at the head from the front and make adjustments so the ears remain symmetrical. You can always take an ear off and fasten it again.

Eyes

1. Now make two indentations with your needle where the eyes will go. This should be in line with the ears. Then felt a tiny wisp of brown down into the hollow. Keep the eye small.

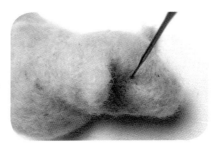

Nose and mouth

1. Felt a tiny brown triangle onto the end of the face with your fine felting needle for a nose and 'draw' a small brown line going down from the centre of the nose.

2. Roll a tiny bit of brown between your fingers into a string about 0.5–1cm long and felt this into the shape of a mouth (for the lamb, add a little pink around the nose and mouth).

Next you have to decide if you are making a lying down sheep or a standing up one.

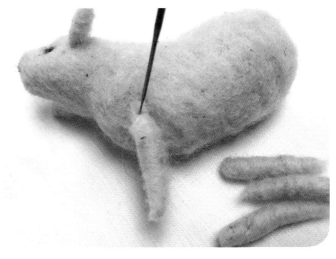

Legs

1. For a standing sheep, wrap the white wool tightly around your medium needle. If you are using the South German Merino or Ryeland Lamb, you will find it easy to wrap as the wool is very 'sticky' like Velcro.

2. When the leg is approx. 3–4cm long and 5–8mm thick, slip it off the needle and felt down a little. Also felt straight into the base at one end so that the sheep can stand on flat feet. Make three others the same.

3. To attach them, tease a little loose wool out of the top (not the flat felted foot part) and attach to the sheep's body slightly to its side. Repeat with all four legs. They will not be fastened properly yet but positioned in the right place.

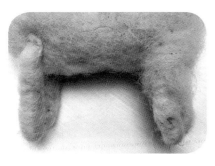

4. Next use a wisp of the white wool and lay it over the outside of the leg's join. Felt it down with your medium needle so that it creates support by being tightly pulled half way around the top of the leg and felted on the inside of the top of the leg under the sheep's body.

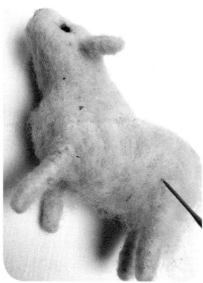

5. For a lying down sheep, bend the legs that you have attached in the middle and felt them down until they tuck in nicely under the sheep and you can see the bent knees on the side. Felt the legs down hard so that the sheep looks as though it is lying down comfortably.

For an even simpler version of a lying down sheep, skip the leg part altogether and just add curls. If they are covering the side of the sheep you won't be able to notice the absence of legs.

Fleece

1. You can leave the sheep like this or add curls. Take small batches of curls and attach the frizzy parts with a fine or medium needle and leave the more curly part hanging down or un-felted.

2. Remember not to pull the curls apart but use scissors to cut them to stop them from becoming frizzy. Work your way from the bottom up, so start around the legs and add layers as you go up towards the head.

3. Use the whiter curls for the lamb and the yellower ones for the ewe.

Tail

1. Finally, for the tail, find a bit of more solid curl, felt it down on your mat before fastening it onto the sheep's backside with your felting needle.

The Nativity: Mary, Joseph and Baby Jesus

I admit that our house is not a Christian one but for many years I have had Mary and Joseph and their little donkey make their journey to the stable. Being German, the time of Advent is very important to me and I have fond memories of it: a time of frosty nights and days, the first snow, anticipation of the holidays, good food, Glühwein, Christmas markets, a sense of love, sharing and togetherness. Christmas itself is a quiet affair in Germany, time spent cosying up at home with the family and no venturing out into the world.

I came across the story book *A Light in the Lantern: Stories for Advent* by Georg Dreissig when my children were toddlers and I loved the idea of reading them a short story each night during Advent and the following morning they would find a symbol of that story in their advent calendar to put on the seasonal table where Mary and Joseph had started their journey. The story follows Mary and Joseph on their way to Bethlehem. It is told in such a playful and warm way that we decided to adopt the lessons of kindness, patience, love and sharing especially during the time of Advent. It also meant that my children raced down the stairs in the morning to find a little handmade item rather than chocolate in a commercially mass-produced advent calendar. And though after years of reading the same book each year, the children knew the stories off by heart, the excitement never seemed to cease and later the older children read to the younger ones.

Many projects in my book can become part of that winter story, such as mice, rabbits, robins, spiders, sheep, donkeys, angels, etc.

Mary

YOU WILL NEED

For Mary

2g flesh-pink South American Merino wool tops

4g white wool batts (e.g. South German Merino, Shetland, Gotland, Fox Sheep)

4–5g blue New Zealand Merino wool batts

1g red New Zealand Merino wool batts

1g black or dark wool batts or top (I used New Zealand Merino wool batts)

2 x 30cm pipe cleaner

Strong thread

Coarse and medium felting needles

Felting mat

Sharp scissors

The finished figure is 8–10cm tall.

Body and arms

1. Make the head according to the instructions (see p 32) using 2g of flesh-pink Merino top and 4g of white wool batts (p 28) until you have covered the arms with flesh pink. Do not cut the end of the pipe cleaner off but keep the full length.

2. When the head and arms are finished, bend the end of the pipe cleaner into a loop of about 5cm, and fasten it by twisting the end around the main pipe cleaner. Then bend it upwards so that the loop becomes the base and allows the figure to stand unaided.

3. Next use the red wool and wrap it around the upper body, then felt it down with your coarse or medium needle.

4. Take most of the blue wool (leaving aside 1g or a generous pinch) and flatten it out with your hands and pull a hole into the centre that will fit over Mary's head.

5. Arrange it so that the wool reaches beyond the bottom of the base and can be tucked into the inside of the base later.

6. Now felt the sleeves. For this, arrange the sleeve so that the hand is exposed, then use your coarse felting needle and stab along the underarm on your felting mat, making sure that the blue wool fits snugly around Mary's arm.

7. Turn over and felt the other side. Repeat two to three times until you have felted a seam. Repeat on the other arm. You will not be felting the blue wool down anywhere else for the moment.

8. Use your scissors and cut the blue wool along the seam you have felted so that the sleeve is closed under the arm. Cut all the way to the body, giving the arm full movement. Repeat on the other side.

9. Next use the medium needle and make sure the sleeve looks neat around the arm, covering any thin areas or felting down any wisps that are sticking out.

10. The blue cut part of the cloak that will stick out by the sides needs to be felted into the body so use your coarse needle to do this. This will create a waistline.

11. Felt more of the blue body down but make sure that you keep an area open where baby Jesus can fit in, as well as leaving the red cover on show. For now, if you can put the tip of your finger inside, it will be enough space.

12. Now tuck the bottom of the cloak inside the loop at the bottom and felt it down with your coarse needle. Be careful not to stab your fingers, as it will be hard to lay the figure onto the felting mat.

13. The next part is optional: you can use the remaining blue wool and push it inside the frame. This will give you more of a base to felt on and will completely cover the pipe cleaner inside. Felt down the blue cloak more firmly if you wish. This will make your figure more robust.

Hair

1. Use a pinch of the black hair and cover part of the head, focusing first on framing the face with hair.

2. Felt it on lightly and use more wool to cover the whole head. Leave some longer strands hanging down the back and sides.

Joseph

YOU WILL NEED

For Joseph

- 2g flesh-pink South American Merino wool tops
- 4g white wool batts (I used South German Merino, Shetland, Gotland, Fox Sheep)
- 5g medium to dark brown wool batts (such as Mountain Sheep – dark brown, Russian Karakul – caramel-coloured or dyed brown New Zealand Merino)
- Pinch of dark brown wool batt (such as dyed brown New Zealand Merino) for the cap (optional)
- 1g brown/grey Wensleydale curls or grey Herdwick Sheep top (depending how old you want Joseph to be)
- 2 x 30cm pipe cleaner
- 30cm length of brown yarn
- 15cm-long twig (for Joseph's stick)

Strong thread

2g brown/grey or just brown wool batts for Joseph's legs (I used South German Merino but you can also use Milksheep, Portuguese Merino, both dark brown, or Russian Karakul (caramel colour) to coordinate with Joseph's cloak

1g dark brown or black for the boots (I used Stone Sheep natural black but the colour for the cap will work too)

Coarse and medium felting needles

Felting mat

Sharp scissors

The finished figure is 10–12cm tall.

Make the head according to the instructions for figures using flesh-pink Merino top and white wool batts (p 28) until you have covered the arms (p 32) with flesh pink. Do not cut the end of the pipe cleaner off but keep the full length.

You have two options now:

1. Make Joseph a long cloak similar to Mary's (the easier option).
2. Make two legs for Joseph and use the twig to balance him (slightly more complicated).

These instructions for making Joseph can also be used to make shepherds of varying sizes.

OPTION 1

When the head and arms are finished, bend the end of the pipe cleaner into a loop of about 5cm and fasten it by twisting the end around the main pipe cleaner. Then bend it upwards so that the loop becomes the base and allows the figure to stand unaided.

Bend the pipe cleaner base so that Joseph stands slightly taller than Mary.

From here we follow similar instructions as for making Mary's cloak (p 149):

Cloak

1. Take most of the larger quantity brown wool (leave 1g or a generous pinch), flatten it out with your hands and pull a hole into the centre that will fit over Joseph's head.

2. Arrange it so that the wool reaches beyond the bottom of the base and can be tucked into the inside of the base later.

3. To felt the sleeves, start with the exposed hand and use your coarse felting needle to stab along the underarm on your felting mat, making sure that the brown wool fits snugly around Joseph's arm.

4. Turn over and felt the other side. Repeat two to three times until you have felted a seam. Repeat on the other arm. You will not be felting the brown wool down anywhere else for the moment.

5. Use your scissors and cut the brown wool below the seam you have felted so that the sleeve is closed under the arm. Cut all the way to the body, giving the arm full movement. Repeat on the other side.

6. Next use the medium needle and make sure the sleeve looks neat around the arm, covering any thin areas and felting down any wisps that are sticking out.

7. The brown cut part of the cloak that will stick out by the sides needs to be felted into the side of the body and it's best to use your coarse needle for this, which will also create a waist line.

8. Felt more of the brown body down and give Joseph a straighter shape than Mary's.

9. Now tuck the bottom of the cloak inside the frame/loop and felt it down with your coarse needle. Be careful not to stab your fingers as it will be hard to lay the figure onto the felting mat.

10. As an optional extra, you can push the remaining brown wool inside the frame. This will give you more of a base to felt on and will completely cover the pipe cleaner inside. If you felt it down more firmly, it will be sturdier for a small child to play with.

11. Tie the length of yarn around Joseph's waist and secure it with a knot or bow at the front. Then cut off the excess.

12. Now jump to 'Hair and beard' instructions.

OPTION 2

Legs

1. Cut a 15cm length off the main pipe cleaner and bend the remaining body pipe cleaner up and round the centre of the cut length. These will be the legs.

2. Wrap the body length pipe cleaner around the centre of the leg pipe cleaner a couple more times and secure it, winding it around the lower body two or three times. Then cut off the excess. The distance between the neck and the join of the leg pipe cleaner should measure about 3–3.5cm.

3. Start wrapping your brown/grey or brown wool around a leg pipe cleaner, starting about 0.5cm away from the end. Wrap a thin layer of about 1cm wide and then fold the end of the pipe cleaner in on itself to hide the sharp end and continue wrapping up the leg from the foot.

4. Tease the wool apart as you go along to create thin layers that 'stick' together like Velcro. Wrap the wool like a ribbon, keeping it flat.

5. When you reach the top of the leg, wrap a few strands of wool around the lower body.

6. If the strand of wool tears, just start again wrapping in the same direction. Make sure you wrap the wool tightly so it does not come off. Repeat with the other leg. Leave enough wool so that you can build another layer on for the trousers. Leave the foot part thinner. Now use your medium or fine needle and felt the legs down a little.

Boots

1. Bend the ends of the pipe cleaner in about 1–2cm to make feet. Use your black or dark brown wool and add a layer on the foot, heel and ankle. Use your fine needle and felt the wool down at the front of the boot/shoe to make it round, then underneath to make it flat and finally, around the ankle to help shape the heel and fasten it onto the leg.

2. Repeat with the other foot. Make sure you have both legs the same length; if they're not, now is the chance to adjust the bend in the foot. You can always compensate with the amount of wool you use for the boot.

Cloak

1. Take two-thirds of the wool you're using for this and flatten it with your hands into a square of approx. 12 x 12cm and then make a hole in the centre. Lay it flat on your felting mat and felt a straight line along two opposite edges. Fold the wispy ends on both edges inwards and create a neat finish by felting them down with your coarse needle. Felt all over by stabbing the needle at an angle into the wool to create a slightly matted fabric but don't overwork it. Felt on both sides, remembering to lift off the mat regularly. You should end up with a square piece that has two neat edges opposite each other.

2. Slip this over Joseph's head so that the neat edges are at the front and back and the not-so-neat edges are covering his arms.

3. Now felt the sleeves. For this, expose the hand and then use your coarse felting needle and stab along the underarm on your felting mat, making sure that the brown wool fits snugly around Joseph's arm.

4. Turn it over and felt the other side. Repeat two to three times until you have felted a seam. Repeat on the other arm. You will not be felting the brown wool down anywhere else for the moment.

5. Next use your scissors and cut the brown wool below the seam you have felted so that the sleeve is closed under the arm. Cut all the way to the body, giving the arm full movement. Repeat on the other side.

6. Next use the medium needle and make sure the sleeve looks neat around the arm, covering any thin areas by felting any wisps that are sticking out.

7. The brown cut part of the cloak will stick out by the sides and needs to be felted into the side of the body. Use your coarse needle to do this, which will create a waistline.

8. Felt more of the brown body down and make sure the cloak is long enough to go down to Joseph's knees. Shape both the cloak and Joseph by stabbing the coarse needle in the area around his neck, under the arm and all around.

9. Then tie the yarn around his middle and secure with a knot or bow and trim any excess.

Hair and beard

1. When you have completed either option for Joseph, it's time to make the hair. If you have curls, pull the wool so the hair will be more wavy rather than curly. Fasten small strands of wool to Joseph's head, concentrating first on framing his face, and don't worry if his hair looks too long to start with as you can trim it later. Then fasten some hair onto his chin too for a beard.

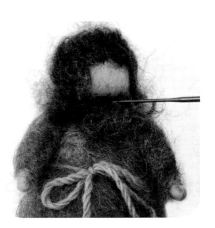

Cap

1. If you want to give Joseph a cap, flatten a pinch of brown into a shape of approx. 7cm in diameter. Felt this down on your mat with a coarse needle, tucking the wispy edges into the centre and reducing the shape to approx. 5cm diameter.

2. Felt on both sides into a little disc so it holds its own shape and is evenly felted (no thin patches). Place this onto Joseph's head.

3. Then, using your coarse or medium needle, only felt about 1cm from the sides of the disc into the head of Joseph, fastening the brown disc on, thereby creating a rim. You won't have to stab into the top of the cap. This part will automatically shape around the top of the head.

4. Finally, bend Joseph's hand in so that he can hold the stick and balance him by adjusting the legs and stick. If you wish, you can glue it on.

Baby Jesus

These instructions can also be used for any baby, for example bud babies or babies for fairies. They can also be scaled up and can be popular for a child to have as a pocket baby.

Baby Jesus is only tiny, just big enough for Mary to hold him in her arms.

YOU WILL NEED

For Baby Jesus

Pinch of cream or white wool batts (I used lanolin-rich organic South German Merino)

Wisp of flesh-pink New Zealand Merino wool batts

Tiny wisp of brown wool (even 1cm of wool yarn will be suitable)

Medium and fine felting needles

Felting mat

The finished figure is 2.5–3cm long.

Body

1. Roll three-quarters of the cream wool into a short sausage. Felt down the wispy ends and give it a few stabs all over to firm it up, until it measures about 3cm.

Head

1. Then use a wisp of the flesh-pink wool and wrap one third of the shape towards the top. You only need one side of the pink to look even but needle felt all of it down with a medium or fine needle. Decide which part looks the neatest.

Blanket

1. Use the remaining white wool (or enough) to cover the baby's head and come down to wrap over his body. It should overlap the cream body and, once felted on, become one continuous wrap, only showing a little round pink face. If too much pink is showing, add a little more cream.

2. Felt the shape further down so it looks more like a kidney shape. This is easily achieved by stabbing your fine needle deeply into the line between the face/chin and cream wool. It will not only bend the shape inward but also define the head more.

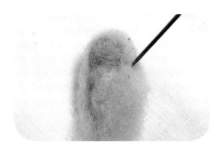

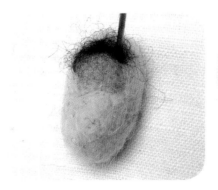

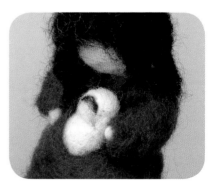

Hair

1. Finally, take a tiny wisp of the dark brown for the hair and with your fine needle tuck a few fibres into the top of the hood.

2. Make any adjustments necessary to keep the kidney shape and define the head shape.

3. Tuck the baby into Mary's cloak supported by her arms.

Robin

The robin, such an important little bird in our western European gardens: a friendly little fellow who has become the symbol of British winters and whom we associate with Christmas. However, I notice the robins all year round. They are quite bold in their interaction with us humans and come close when a juicy worm is in the offing whilst we're digging the garden. They also seem to have habitual places where they greet us with their distinct song. I always stop and say hello as I can't help but feel a little happier when seeing their bright chest and bright eyes. The robin we are making here is a fluffed up little chap keeping himself warm.

YOU WILL NEED

8g white Shetland or Gotland wool batts
1g orange (here orange variegated or muted orange) New Zealand wool batts
1g Countrysheep wool batts
Wisp of black wool top for the beak but also eyes (if not using the glue-in glass eyes)
Coarse and medium felting needles
Felting mat
Glue

Optional
6mm glue-in glass eyes
5cm-long black wire bird legs

This robin is 7cm tall including legs, and 8cm long, including tail.

Body

1. Take most of the white wool, keeping aside a small pinch for possible patching up later. Roll this into a medium firm ball. You should be able to squeeze it still but it needs to be firm enough so you can stab a needle into it. If in any doubt, go for a tighter ball.

2. Using your coarse needle, start by stabbing the loose wisps into the ball so that it will hold its own shape. The ball should measure about 6–7cm in diameter now.

3. Stab the ball all over to tighten it up and cover with the remaining white wool if there are uneven parts or cracks. Even without imperfections, still use up all the wool. The ball should shrink down by a maximum of 1cm.

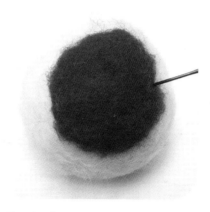

4. Take three-quarters of your orange wool and flatten it into a round shape with your fingers. At the same time take your brown wool, keep a wisp aside, and turn it into a round flat piece. The brown should be slightly larger than the orange. Use your coarse needle and give both orange and brown wool discs a few stabs on your mat to flatten them down further, trying to give them neat edges.

5. Then lay the orange onto the white ball and felt it down with your coarse needle onto the white surface. You should have an orange disc on the white ball. You may have to reshape the white ball again as it will have been affected by adding the orange.

6. Next add the brown by first felting down the part that will touch the orange. This part will form the top and side of the head and the eyes will go where all three colours meet.

7. Next stab the needle along the sides where the wings are. Keep the end loose for the moment, this part will become the tail.

8. Fasten more of the brown onto the white by stabbing the needle across the back of the robin. Then fold the brown so that it makes a pointy end. You may have to tease it out with your fingers slightly.

9. Lay the pointy tail end onto your mat and felt down with your coarse needle. Felt on both sides. Cover any thin patches with the wisps of brown you kept aside or maybe to even out some unsymmetrical areas.

10. As we only have a soft shape, now is the opportunity to turn the ball into more of a bird shape. Start by making the side of the head smaller by stabbing your needle into the 'eye' area where the orange, brown and white meet.

11. Next flatten down the back by stabbing your needle along the brown from head to tail. You may find that you need to change from your coarse to your medium felting needle now when giving the bird an all-round makeover.

. . . .

Eyes

1. If you are using glue-in eyes, use your coarse needle and sink it all the way from one eye across the head to the other side and move it in and out a few times, making sure the needle goes in all the way to the shaft. This will create two big holes where the pins of the glass eyes can sink in.

2. Check they are symmetrical before applying a dab of glue to fasten them in. Remember the eyes are positioned where the brown, white and orange meet.

3. If you choose to needle felt the eyes, take two equal wisps of the black wool and turn them into two equal-sized balls by first using your fingers and then giving them a few stabs with your needle.

4. The size of each eye before fastening onto the robin should be no larger than 8mm.

5. Secure the black ball onto the robin (where the brown, orange and white meet) by stabbing a few times around the base of the ball, thereby keeping it round rather than flat.

6. Repeat on the other side then add a tiny wisp of white for reflection points.

. . . .

Beak

1. Flatten a wisp of black wool with your fingers and fold it in half. Then roll it up so the straight folded edge becomes the pointy end of the beak and the opposite end stays fluffy.

2. Felt down with your medium needle on your mat into a pointy small beak of 1cm long. Open up the wispy ends and felt them down onto the bird in line with the eyes. You can reduce the beak in size by stabbing your medium needle lengthways into the beak towards the face.

3. If too much of the black on the face at the end of the beak is showing, use tiny wisps of brown or orange and cover the black up a little.

Legs

1. If you are not using wire legs, felt the bottom of the robin flat so it can sit without falling over.

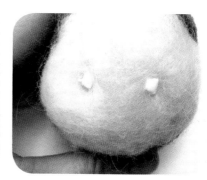

2. If you are using legs, bend the top half of the leg in towards the toes.

3. Then make two holes underneath the robin toward the tail as follows: the robin gains his stability by the bend in the legs going forwards into the body, therefore make your holes by inserting your coarse needle at an angle towards the front of the bird. Gently wiggle the needle around and pull it out and push it in again to make a larger hole.

4. Then take the needle out and try putting one of the legs into the hole you have created. Repeat this on the other side. Remember the legs are bendable so if they are not standing straight you don't necessarily have to change the hole. You may be able to adjust the legs later.

5. Put a little dab of glue on each hole, insert the legs and leave your robin to dry standing on the legs. Do not move it until you are certain the glue has dried. You can add a little white wool if you have some available still to cover the join between the legs and the body to give the impression of tiny 'bloomers'.

6. The wire legs are very versatile. Not only can you bend them but you can also decorate them by painting them with acrylic paints or wrapping florist tape around, as well as shortening them with wire cutters if necessary.

Baubles

Baubles are a great classic Christmas tree decoration. I have added this project in the book as knowing how to make a round shape can be useful for other projects: pom-poms, balls, or the beginning of other 3D projects, such as birds. So bear this in mind when you make a bauble: use these instructions for other decorations around the year!

YOU WILL NEED

For the red bauble (left)

15g of wool batt (I used red New Zealand Merino)

1g of contrasting colour (I used turquoise variegated New Zealand mix)

Length of ribbon (I used 60cm of curling gift ribbon, a great way to recycle these from the previous Christmas!)

Coarse and medium felting needle

Felting mat

Darning needle (to fit the ribbon)

This makes a medium to firm ball shape of approx. 8cm

Bauble shape

1. First take a good pinch of the main wool and put to one side. We are keeping this for later to cover any unevenness or cracks in the ball.

2. Roll the larger amount of wool into a ball. I do this by rolling it up and in on itself, starting with a small core and spreading the wool over the core while rolling it up. You end up with wispy ends, which are the first parts you felt down with your coarse felting needle. This will help to stop the ball from uncurling itself.

3. Next use the needle and felt the wool down evenly all over, always maintaining the round ball shape. If your shape becomes flat, you need to stab the needle where you would naturally squeeze the shape to make it round again. Do not stab more on the flat surface!

4. Similarly, if you have created a hollow or crack, it will not close if you keep stabbing into it. Stab around it to try and close it up. If that is not possible, use some of the spare wool and lay a thin layer on the top and felt it down. Make sure that the layer will cover the area that needs concealing.

5. Remember to sink the needle right into the shape to create a fairly firm ball. It pays to have a more solid shape if you are going to add surface decorations later.

6. As the ball becomes firmer, you may have to change to your medium needle to continue felting it down.

7. Once the desired shape has been achieved, use the remainder of the wool you kept aside to lay over the top, even if there are no areas that need covering.

Adding decoration

1. Decorating your bauble or ball can be done in so many ways: stripes, spots, shapes, pictures etc. I am certain that your imagination will help you design many of your own baubles. Here I will be showing you how to decorate the bauble with strands of wool and spots.

2. To make stripes or swirls, roll your contrasting wool into a strand between your fingers. You can vary the thickness of it by teasing the wool apart, taking care not to tear it.

3. Start by fastening one end of it onto the ball with your coarse or medium needle.

4. Fasten the strand on as you go, continuing to twist it between your fingers if needed. If you come to the end of a strand, start where you finished with a new one. You will be able to create an invisible continuation.

5. To add spots or round, flat shapes, take a wisp of the contrasting wool and flatten it into a disc with your fingers. Then fasten it onto the ball by stabbing it on, concentrating the needle around the edge to make it a clear contrast.

6. Whilst adding detail to the bauble you will have to adjust the ball shape constantly. So not only will you stab the needle into the decorative wool but also all around it to stop grooves and indentations pulling your ball out of shape.

• •

Adding the ribbon

1. The most secure way to fasten the ribbon onto the bauble is by going into the top of it with a darning needle (ribbon threaded onto it), all the way through the bottom.

2. Come out and go back up the same way but a couple of millimetres next to where the needle first went in.

3. Come out at the top and pull both ends of the ribbon into an equal length and knot to your required length.

4. It is inevitable that you will pull the bottom of the bauble in during this process. Just tease the wool a little in that area.

5. You may be able to felt teased-out fibres over that area. That should make the ribbon indentation disappear again.

Christmas pudding bauble

Bauble shape

1. Make a bauble shape in exactly the same way as for the red bauble (p 161) but use the brown main wool batts.

Adding decoration

1. Next use half of the white wool and lay it over the top of the bauble. Felt this down with your medium needle so that it looks as though the cream is running off the top of the brown ball (pudding). Add more white as and where required. You could have one side where the cream (white wool) is 'running off' more.

YOU WILL NEED

For the Christmas pudding bauble

15g rich brown wool batts (I used Countrysheep but brown Mountain Sheep and Portuguese Merino as well as Milksheep would be suitable too)

1g red wool batts (New Zealand Merino)

1g green wool batts (e.g. variegated green New Zealand mix)

2g white wool batts (Cape Merino but Gotland or Shetland would work too)

1 x length of ribbon (I used 60cm of red raffia)

Coarse and medium felting needles

Felting mat

Darning needle (to fit the ribbon)

Small sharp scissors

This makes a medium to firm ball shape of approx. 8cm.

Holly leaves

1. Then split the green wool in half. Lay one half of it onto your felting mat and felt it flat into a leaf shape. Keep lifting the piece off the mat so it does not get fastened onto it.

You can make stiffer leaves following the instructions on page 107.

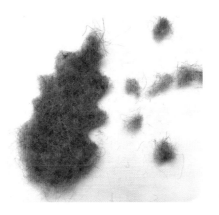
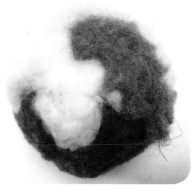

2. Then cut half circles out of the edge of the leaf going all the way round. This will give it the distinct look of a holly leaf. Repeat with the other half of the green wool.

3. Position one leaf on top of the bauble and felt it down, concentrating the needle around the edge of the leaf to make the pointy features more distinct against the wool underneath. You can leave the tips of the leaf unfelted to give it more of a 3D effect. Felt the second leaf on in the same way.

Berries

1. Use three wisps of the red wool and roll one into a tight little ball. Holding the ball tight in your fingers, lay it on top of the bauble, still holding it, so it does not pop open and felt it down with your medium needle, only stabbing into the edge of the berry and the top of the bauble.

2. Doing this will not only fasten the berry onto the bauble but it will also make sure it maintains its round, bulbous shape. Repeat this process twice more to create three berries sitting on top of the pudding.

3. Neaten up your pudding bauble by making sure that all the features added (white, green and red) have a nice contrasting edge against the wool underneath.

Adding the ribbon

1. Add the ribbon to hang your Christmas pudding bauble exactly as for the red bauble (p 162).

Frequently asked questions

When needle felting, do you fluff things up?

The needle felting process actually does the opposite. You are compressing the wool down and though a finished feltie looks 'fluffy' or soft, comparing it to the un-felted wool it is a lot less fluffy. It will also become more solid as the fibres tangle together and it will reduce in size.

Why do you often use white wool as a core?

Coloured or dyed wool is usually more expensive whereas white core wool is cheaper. As the core is often the largest quantity used, it is more economical to make the core from the cheaper wool and use the more expensive coloured wool on the top. White is the most neutral and easy to cover with any colour later on. However, on small projects it makes little difference using white as a core.

Can needles become blunt?

Yes, they can, though you have to do an awful lot of felting for this to happen. My needles usually break before they get blunt.

Can needles break?

Yes, they can. I break most of my needles if I hit a wire or pipe cleaner or if I use a fine needle on a fairly solid project. Needles can also break if you put a strain on them going in and out of the wool by making a 'curved' movement. Try and keep your wrist stiff and let the movement come from your arm. Go straight in and straight out.

Can I straighten bent needles?

Once needles are bent it is virtually impossible to get them exactly straight again. If you try to straighten them, they will most likely break. This is because they are made from steel that has little flexibility.

How can I tell my different needle sizes apart?

Unless you have a wire gauge measuring tool this can be tricky. Some types of needles are longer or shorter depending on their size. The longer the needle, the coarser. As an experienced needle felter you will be able to tell them apart by looking at the barbed end. The easiest way to tell them apart is by stabbing them into a loosely rolled-up ball of wool and if they felt well, they are more likely to be coarser; if little happens they will be finer. Similarly stab into an already firmly felted object and the needle that does not even sink into it will be coarser; the one that still goes in will be the finer one.

Why do my felties always stay soft?

There may be several reasons for this:
1. You are not using a coarse enough needle to efficiently tangle up the fibres.
2. You are not giving it enough stabs.
3. You are not sinking the needle in deep enough. If you only sink the needle into a shape about 1cm, all you will be felting is the surface up to 1cm deep.

If you want to achieve a firmer felt, stab the needle continuously into the core. When you only want to add surface details, stop going all the way in and just work on the surface.

How do I shorten features such as ears, legs, beaks etc?

If you have already attached those parts and you want to shorten them, there are two ways:
1. Stab your needle lengthways into the part that needs shortening towards the main body of your feltie. Basically, you continue to felt the part by going in at a shallow angle, therefore reducing the size that way.
2. If your part is already firmly felted and there is little give, use scissors to trim into shape. You can always add wool again to cover any uneven parts that have occurred as a result.

How do I store my wool or felted decorations?

The biggest enemy of all things woolly are probably clothes moths. These are the little silvery moths that shy away from light (most moths will seek out light). They are only a pest if you have male and female together as the female will find woolly materials to lay her eggs in. When the eggs hatch, the larvae can stay in the wool for up to two and a half years before turning into moths. They are the ones that will eat the wool for food. They can be hard to spot but you will spot the eaten-off ends of wool as they are like a cut edge. The best is to have preventative measures in place. Moths do not like daylight or disturbance so make sure you keep your wool or felties in a light and airy place and move them around occasionally. Or keep them in an airtight bag or container. Put mothballs with a strong scent into the bag or container (you can get cedar balls or more natural sachets that are based on essential oils and lavender).

Once you have an infestation, you need to act more severely. However, if you have a large freezer you can kill all moths and larvae by putting the woolly items into it for a couple of days if you prefer not to use chemicals (moth killing sprays etc). You can also buy moth traps which attract the male moth (the one that usually flies) and so the female moth (the one that usually hops around the ground) is harmless. The traps need to be replaced regularly.

My finished feltie never looks exactly like the one I have tried to copy. What am I doing wrong?

Nothing! Needle felting is amazing in the way that everybody puts their own fingerprint onto their creations and the nature of the wool in its responsiveness and tactility enables you to make something that is truly unique.

Needle felting is different in that respect to sewing, knitting, card making, cross stitch etc. If you are following a pattern, you will likely end up with a carbon copy of the project. Not so in needle felting! This is what I love about it. None of my projects always look the same! Enjoy the creative freedom and let your own style develop.

I know something does not look right (face, shape, proportion etc) but the more I look at it, the less I can see what I need to change. What should I do?

First of all, walk away from it for a bit and then come back with fresh eyes! Sometimes we get too locked into a project that we stop seeing it objectively. If you are struggling with the symmetry of a face, for example, look at it in a mirror. That will often give you another perspective and you can see where you have to tweak things. Look at real life pictures of what you are trying to make for a reality check. We all form images in our mind that are not true to nature.

Sometimes it helps asking a friend (one you trust) who appreciates the work that has gone into your project, to get their constructive feedback. And sometimes you just have to be kind to yourself and stop being over-critical or perfectionist!

Resources

England

THE MAKERSS
www.themakerss.co.uk
info@themakerss.co.uk

For all needle felting supplies, kits, video tutorials, accessories (such as glue-in eyes and bird legs), tools, workshops, talks on needlefelting, retreats, needle felting events and books.

The Makerss,
Unit 19,
Nailsworth Mills Estate,
Nailsworth, GL6 0BS
Tel 01453 839454

Facebook:
www.facebook.com/themakerss.co.uk
and
www.facebook.com/everyoneamaker

Twitter:**@themakerss**
Instagram:**@themakerss**

A resource for all needle felting needs, including supplies, ideas and practical help – over 10,000 members:
www.facebook.com/needlefeltinguk

Canada

BEAR DANCE CRAFTS
Tel: +1 (250) 353 2220
www.beardancecrafts.com
Needle felting materials.

MAPLEROSE
265 Baker Street
Nelson BC
V1L 4H4
Tel: +1 (250) 352 5729
www.maplerose.ca
Needle felting materials.

USA

A CHILD'S DREAM COME TRUE
214-A Cedar Street
Sandpoint
Idaho 83864
Tel: +1 (208) 255 1664
www.achildsdream.com
info@achildsdream.com
Needle felting materials.

PARADISE FIBERS
225 W. Indiana
Spokane, WA 99205
Tel: +1 (509) 536 7746
www.paradisefibers.com
Needle felting materials.

Acknowledgements

My biggest gratitude is as always to my family, husband and four children, who endure hours of absentmindedness, mediocre sofa dinners (when the kitchen table becomes my work space for days on end), short tempered-ness and general lack of presence. I really appreciate that you allow me to fulfil this part of me. Thank you!

Secondly, and on equal par, are my craft editor Christine Kidney and publisher Martin Large. I am very grateful for your encouragement, enthusiasm and belief in me. It has allowed me to find the confidence in doing what I love best: creating and writing! Thank you Christine, for being thorough and not stopping until you are happy! Thank you both for your friendship too!

My gratitude goes to Sophie Buckley who is quietly by my side during every word I write and every project I make. I really appreciate your support.

And of course a big thank you to all of those who work their magic and creative talents on making the book look lovely: Laura Mirjami (photographic styling), Faisal Khouja (photography) and last but by no means least, Lucy Guenot (book design).

My final thanks go to all of you wonderful and amazing needle felting 'addicts' who let me know every day how much you appreciate what I contribute towards spreading the needle felting love. I really don't feel I deserve half of it but you all make me very proud. You all know who you are!

Steffi Stern

More books from Hawthorn Press

Making Needle Felted Animals
Over 20 wild, domestic and imaginary creatures
Steffi Stern, Sophie Buckley

Making Needle Felted Animals is an essential guide for anyone interested in the popular craft of needle felting. Whether you are completely new to needle felting or an experienced felter, this book will have something to offer, from precise instruction to creative inspiration.

Written by two authors expert in making and teaching crafts to students of all ages and abilities, instructions are easy to follow and include practical yet creative ideas to fix common mistakes. The projects arise from a genuine love of the natural world and animals, whether they be family pets or wild creatures. Requiring no experience other than an interest in working and playing with wool, projects progressively build on skills throughout and will transform you into an avid needle-felter in no time at all.

'This book is gorgeous – the animals are so lifelike and appealing – it makes you want to get started straight away.'
Melissa Corkhill, *The Green Parent Magazine*

128pp; 250 x 200mm; paperback; 978-1-907359-46-0

Making the Children's Year
Seasonal Waldorf Crafts with Children
Marije Rowling

Making the Children's Year is a family resource for seasonal crafts with children. Drawing on the creative ethos of Steiner Waldorf education, this is a full-colour second edition of *The Children's Year*, which has been a much-loved favourite for over 30 years. Packed with all kinds of crafts, from papercrafting to building dens, Marije brings the seasons into the home. From beginners to experienced crafters, this book is a gift for parents and adults seeking to make toys that will inspire children and provides a welcome alternative to our throwaway culture.

'I love the sense of the seasons this book provides alongside a wealth of crafting ideas.' Saffia Farr, *Juno Magazine*

240pp; 250 x 200mm; paperback; 978-1-907359-69-9

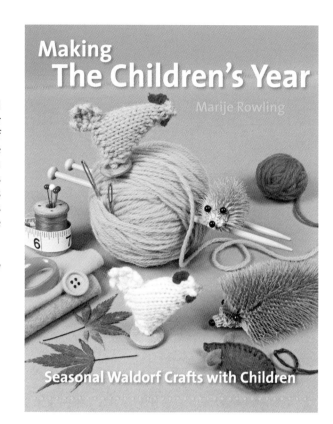

Making Peg Dolls
Margaret Bloom

Coming from the Waldorf handcraft tradition, these irresistible dolls encourage creative play and promote the emotional and imaginative development of young children. Peg dolls can be made from natural materials to reflect the seasonal cycle, favourite fairytales and festivals from around the world. Includes easy to follow, step-by-step instructions for children and crafters of all levels and experience, beautiful colour illustrations and photos, a range of over 60 designs and patterns for peg dolls and an inspiring section on storytelling with peg dolls

192pp; 198 x 208mm; hardback; 978-1-907359-17-0

Making Woodland Crafts
Using green sticks, rods, poles, beads and string
Patrick Harrison

An artwork in its own right, this book provides the basic knowledge and skills to complete a range of both simple and more advanced craft projects, from functional structures to creative outdoor play forms. You'll learn to choose and work your wood effectively, use simple tools, tie knots and develop your own designs to make masks and puppets, night torches, arrows, jewellery, ladders, shelters, chairs for stargazing and much more. This book will teach you all you need to know to make working with wood fun for parents, teachers and children. Step-by-step instructions throughout, with beautiful hand-drawn illustrations.

128pp; 198 x 208mm; hardback; 978-1-907359-37-8

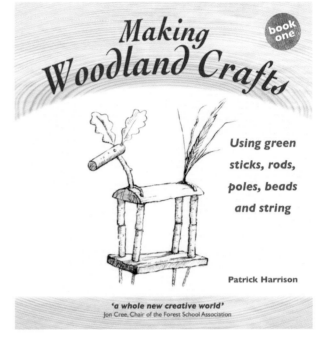

Making Soft Dolls
Simple Waldorf designs to sew and love
Steffi Stern

What is it about dolls that captures the imagination of children and adults around the world? Why do Waldorf dolls have few facial features? This book answers these questions and highlights the power of dolls used for therapeutic purposes, recognising that soft dolls aren't just for children.

Create your own charming dolls' house doll family plus their clothes and accessories. From the simplest rag doll to curly-haired characters, this book gives step-by-step instructions with clear drawings and templates, with simple sewing for beginners, and no sewing machine required. A lovingly hand-made doll makes the perfect present and will be much loved for generations.

128pp; 250 x 200mm; paperback; 978-1-912480-05-0

All Year Round
A calendar of celebration

Ann Druitt, Christine Fynes-Clinton, Marije Rowling

All Year Round is brimming with things to make, activities, stories, poems and songs to share with your family. It is full of well-illustrated ideas for fun and celebration. Observing the round of festivals is an enjoyable way to bring rhythm into children's lives and provide a series of meaningful landmarks to look forward to. Each festival has a special character of its own: participation can deepen our understanding and love of nature and bring a gift to the whole family.

'Delightful illustrations, hundreds of things to make, recipes to enjoy and songs to share, make this book a real family treasury.' The Green Parent

320pp; 250 x 200mm; paperback; 978-1-869891-47-6

Festivals Family and Food
Guide to seasonal celebration

Diana Carey, Judy Large

This family favourite is a unique, well-loved source of stories, recipes, things to make, activities, poems, songs and festivals. Each festival such as Christmas, Candlemas and Martinmas has its own, well-illustrated chapter. There are also sections on Birthdays, Rainy Days, Convalescence and a birthday Calendar. The perfect present for a family, it explores the numerous festivals that children love celebrating.

'Every family should have one.' The Daily Mail

224pp; 250 x 200mm; paperback; 978-0-950706-23-8

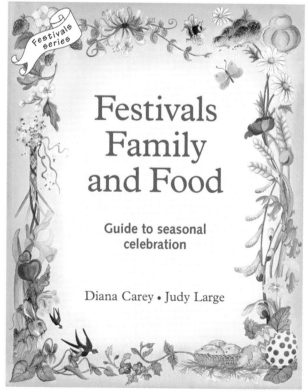

An A-Z Collection of Behaviour Tales
From Angry Ant to Zestless Zebra
Susan Perrow

Susan offers story medicine as a creative strategy to help children age 3–9 years face challenges and change behaviour. Following the alphabet, each undesirable behaviour is identified in the story title: anxious, bullying, demanding, fussy, jealous, loud, obnoxious, uncooperative, and more. The stories, some humorous and some serious, are ideal for parenting, teaching and counselling.

Susan is a storyteller, teacher trainer, parent educator and counsellor and runs therapeutic storytelling workshops all over the world, from China to Africa, Europe to America and across her own sun-burnt land of Australia.

144pp; 234 x 156mm; paperback; 978-1-907359-86-6

The Natural Storyteller
Wildlife Tales for Telling
Georgiana Keable

In these pages you will find over 50 nature stories, chosen to bring both teller and listener closer to their environment. These culturally diverse stories that have stood the test of time will engage young readers, and encourage them to become natural storytellers. The stories are accompanied by tips on telling, story maps, and practical activities.

'The book is life affirming. All of its stories are about taking delight in creation. It is a journey into storytelling as well as story.' Hugh Lupton, award-winning storyteller

272pp; 228 x 186mm; paperback; 978-1-907359-80-4

Findus Food and Fun
Seasonal crafts, recipes and nature activities
Sven Nordqvist, Eva-Lena Larsson, Kennart Danielsson

Pettson, Findus and the muckles have gathered together a whole year's worth of indoor and outdoor activities that can be done using things from around the house. For each month there is something new that can be discovered and explored, invented and made, grown or baked.

Beautifully illustrated and clearly explained, this craft activity book will keep curious children and adults occupied and enchanted all year round.

64pp; 297 x 210mm; hardback; 978-1-907359-34-7

When Findus was Little and Disappeared
Sven Nordqvist

Farmer Pettson and his talking cat Findus live in a red farmhouse, with a henhouse, workshop and tool-shed set among the forests, fields and meadows of rural Sweden. Every picture tells a story, with a fascinating, magical world of tiny creatures. This first book of 10 titles tells the story of when Findus was little and disappeared – and how he came to live with Pettson in the first place.

Children will love these books, and so will parents and grandparents, as they can read them safe in the knowledge that they're gentle, fun, and well-written stories.

'It's not often that we come across books with such immediate and lasting appeal as Sven Nordqvist's 'Findus' series. The stories are ingenious, the characters are quirky and original, and the illustrations are absolutely delightful ... I can't recommend them highly enough. Hurrah for Findus!' Philip Pullman

28pp; 297 x 210mm; hardback; 978-1-903458-83-9

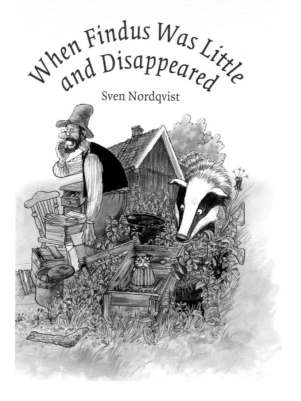

Form Drawing and Colouring
For Fun, Healing and Wellbeing

Angela Lord

This creative form drawing book features fourfold patterns of increasing challenge and complexity. It also offers space for personal creativity, and is a valuable aid to harmonising body and soul. The reader is provided with stunning colourful forms in varying stages of completion to copy, experiment with and develop. This approach offers more creative freedom, as the reader can choose at what level they wish to engage with the forms, be that relaxing drawing or intensely concentrated creation.

96pp; 246 x 189mm; paperback; 978-1-907359-78-1

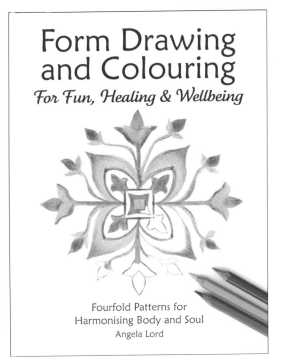

The Children's Forest
Dawn Casey, Anna Richardson, Helen d'Ascoli

An enchanting book where imagination, story and play bring alive the world of the forest. Beautifully illustrated in full colour by Allmut ffrench, this book is full of games, facts, celebrations, craft activities, recipes, foraging, stories and Forest School skills. Organised into the eight Celtic seasons of Imbolc, Spring, Beltane, Summer, Lughnasa, Autumn, Samhain and Winter, each chapter has sections on: The Life of the Forest; Plant Lore; Imaginary Journey; Tree Lore; Activities, crafts and games; Animals; Celebration. The appendices at the end of the book cover woodland skills, safety, the Ogham alphabet, story sources and further resources. *The Children's Forest* is ideal for ages 5–12.

336pp; 250 x 200mm; paperback; 978-1-907359-91-0

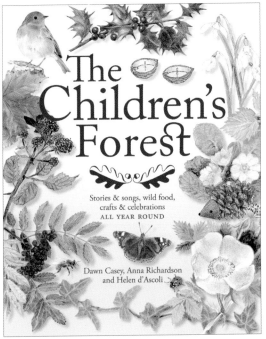

Ordering Books

If you have difficulties ordering Hawthorn Press books from a bookshop, order online at **www.hawthornpress.com** or from our UK distributor
Booksource
50 Cambuslang Road
Glasgow, G32 8NB
Tel: (0845) 370 0063
Email: orders@booksource.net

Hawthorn Press
www.hawthornpress.com